CALLUM MacDONALD & JAN KAPLAN

Prague

IN THE SHADOW OF THE SWASTIKA

A HISTORY OF THE GERMAN OCCUPATION 1939 - 1945

CONTENTS

HITLER OVER PRAGUE   17

THE NEW MASTERS   45

SS CITY   65

THE PALACE OF DEATH   93

THE PRAGUE JEWS   113

OCCUPATIONAL HAZARDS   135

THE HOUR HAS COME   161

AFTERMATH   195

APPENDIX   209

REFERENCES   210

ACKNOWLEDGEMENTS   215

MELANTRICH Publishers

COPYRIGHT © 1995 Callum MacDonald
and Jan Kaplan, Melantrich

All rights reserved. No part of this book may be reproduced in
any form or by any means without the prior written permission of
the publisher

ISBN 80-7023-211-0

President Emil Hácha and Adolf Hitler at Prague Castle on 16 March 1939

> 'It was a great moment in world history when the Führer of the new Reich stood in the Castle of Prague. The foundations were laid for a new order, and a new future was offered to the country and its people.'
>
> KARL HERMANN FRANK

CHAPTER ONE
Hitler over Prague

Hitler surveying Prague from the window of Prague Castle

To Ala, Kathy and Clare.
CALLUM MacDONALD

*To Krystyna and in memory
of my parents.*
JAN KAPLAN

Front cover: The Petschek Palace – Headquarters of the Prague Gestapo – a reconstruction from the documentary film 'SS – 3; The Assassination of Reinhard Heydrich', courtesy of Kaplan Productions

Back cover: Prague, 5 May 1945. German Police in front of the National Museum on Wenceslas Square

PAGE I: During the German occupation, Prague's Municipal House was frequently used for staging propaganda displays such as this exhibition of Nazi architecture advertised above the main entrance

PAGE II–III: Národní třída (National Avenue) in March 1939. A group of SS soldiers are waiting for a tram. On the right, a billboard announces the imminent change from left to right hand drive imposed by the Germans

PAGE IV–V: The 'Deutsches Haus' – the Nazi social and cultural centre on Na Příkopě Street. Next door swastikas hang over the Prague branch of the Thomas Cook Travel agency which was condemned by the Germans as a front for Anglo-French subversion

PAGE VI–VII: A huge 'V' for victory sign on the Municipal House was a part of a German attempt to take over the successful British propaganda campaign of 1941. On the street below Prague residents queue for their cigarette ration

PAGE VIII–IX: A wartime ice hockey match at Prague's Štvanice stadium

PAGE X: Prague, 15 March 1939. An announcement by the commander of the German occupation forces General Blaskowitz stating that by the order of the Führer he has assumed total power

TITLE PAGE: Celetná Street festooned with swastikas

PAGE XIII: A Prague policeman directs traffic during a wartime blackout

PAGE XIV–XV: Prague Castle 15 March 1939. German troops march into the First Courtyard

IT BEGAN, as it was to end, with a radio announcement. On 15 March 1939, at 04:30, the Prague broadcasting station issued a dramatic communique from the State President and the Minister of Defence: 'German Army infantry and aircraft are beginning the occupation of the territory of the Republic at 06:00. The slightest resistance will cause the most unforeseen consequences and lead to the intervention becoming utterly brutal. All commanders have to obey the orders of the occupying Army. The various units of the Czech Army are being disarmed. Military and civil aeroplanes must remain on their aerodromes and none must attempt to take to the air. Prague will be occupied at 06:30.' Further official announcements appealed for calm and ordered the people to go about their normal business. The occupation was the culmination of a long Nazi campaign against Czechoslovakia which was regarded by Hitler as part of German 'living space.' At the Munich conference of September 1938 he secured the Sudetenland with its German-speaking population when the British Prime Minister, Neville Chamberlain, intervened to prevent war. After Munich, the Czechoslovak State President, Eduard Beneš, was forced into exile and the new government adopted a policy of subservience to Nazi Germany. But Hitler was determined to destroy what remained of Czechoslovakia. As he explained to his senior military commanders, there would be no need for fighting: 'All I ask of you is that you have the armed forces ready to march. No mobilization. No unnecessary expense. The Czechs may squeal, but we will have our hands on their throats before they can shout. And anyway, who will come to help them?'

In March 1939 Hitler pressured the Slovaks into demanding independence and Nazi protection. At the same time, Germans in Prague and other cities rioted. Berlin Radio proclaimed that peace and order had broken down and that German citizens were experiencing a reign of terror. This was the excuse for military action. Around the Czech borders, long columns of German Army vehicles were already moving into position. On 14 March, in an attempt to resolve the crisis, the State President, Emil Hácha, made a hurried train journey to Berlin. Arriving at the Anhalter Station at 22:40, he was kept waiting in the Adlon Hotel while the Führer watched a romantic film entitled *Ein Hoffnungsloser Fall* (A Hopeless Case). It was an appropriate epitaph for the Czech state. At 01:00 on 15 March, Hácha was finally summoned to the Reichschancellory. Ushered into the presence of Hitler, he was treated to a crude display of Nazi brutality. Hácha's plaintive appeal on behalf of his people was cut short by an impatient Führer who warned him that the German Army was ready to march. A peaceful occupation would guarantee the Czechs 'autonomy and a certain measure of national freedom'. Resistance would mean extermination and total destruction.

Hácha was given time to contemplate these alternatives. Sent into an anteroom with the commander of the German Luftwaffe,

Hermann Göring, and the Foreign Minister, Joachim von Ribbentrop, he was presented with a paper requesting Hitler to take the Czech people under the protection of the Reich. According to Göring, unless Hácha signed, hundreds of bombers would reduce Prague to ashes within a few hours. Hácha, an old and sick man, fainted and had to be revived with an injection of dextrose and vitamins from Hitler's personal physician, Dr Morell. Worn out by constant bullying, the Czech President finally capitulated and at 03:55 signed the fateful document in the presence of Hitler. The communiqué, a masterpiece of Nazi mendacity, read: 'The conviction was unanimously expressed on both sides that the aim of all efforts must be the safeguarding of calm, order, and peace in this part of Central Europe. The Czechoslovak President declared that, in order to serve this object and to achieve ultimate pacification, he confidently placed the fate of the Czech people and country in the hands of the Führer of the German Reich. The Führer accepted this declaration and expressed his intention of taking the Czech people under the protection of the German Reich and of guaranteeing them an autonomous development of their ethnic life as suited their character.' Events were to show what this ambiguous pledge by Hitler was really worth. Informing the government in Prague by telephone, Hácha claimed that he had sacrificed the state to save the nation. The first German

A German sentry keeps watch over the conquered city on the Moldau

troops, from the SS guard battalion, Leibstandarte Adolf Hitler, had already crossed the border hours before to occupy Moravská-Ostrava.

Hácha's hurried departure for Berlin, cancelling an official visit to the opera, left Prague prey to rumour and uncertainty. Despite Nazi provocations, however, the capital remained calm. On the night of 14 March, local Germans tried to start a riot in the city centre but the Czechs refused to be provoked. An icy wind swept the streets and the demonstrators soon dispersed. By midnight all that remained was a group of rowdy teenagers taunting a few unresponsive Czech policemen near the Deutsches Haus (German House) in Na Příkopě Street. Despite the tension of the previous days, few Czechs predicted what was to come, believing that Hácha's trip prefigured new political concessions by a government that had repeatedly demonstrated its subservience to Berlin. The population of Prague went to bed in a nervous but hopeful mood. The radio announcement before dawn next morning came as a bombshell. Within hours foreign embassies were besieged by terrified people, Czechs, Jews, anti-Nazi refugees, who had good reason to fear the arrival of Hitler's army. George Kennan was an official at the American Legation. As dawn broke, he was faced with the first asylum seekers, two 'dishevelled men, ash-pale with fear' who had been 'Czech spies in Germany . . . and were known to the local Gestapo'. Their 'faces were twitching and their lips trembling' when he turned them away. They were followed by 'two German Social Democrats, fugitives from the Reich' who seemed 'dazed with terror'. Within hours the first suicides had taken place.

The leading German troops, from Army Group Three under General Blaskowitz, reached Prague at 09:00. The advancing columns had been delayed by a blizzard and a series of embarrassing mechanical breakdowns. As they moved through the streets amidst the swirling snow, they were cheered by groups of jubilant local Germans who gave the Hitler salute or waved swastika flags. As for the Czechs, some 'broke down and wept; some abandoned themselves to impotent rage, some rushed shouting abuse at the German troops'. In Wenceslas Square, a large number of people, many of them in tears, sang the National Anthem. Others reacted with apparent indifference, ignoring the heavily armed soldiers who had suddenly appeared in their city. The main German objectives were the airfield at Ruzyně, the War Ministry buildings in Prague-Dejvice and the Hradčany Castle high above Prague, the residence of the Czech President. By 09:30 the troops had seized all

German troops force their way through a crowd of angry Czechs

The Nazi columns were delayed by embarrassing mechanical breakdowns. The signal truck on the left is towing a staff car

these positions and deployed field guns on the castle hill to cover the city. Some vehicles lost their way in the blizzard. Kennan found an armoured car blocking Nerudova Street while the driver asked directions from the Italian Legation: 'A crowd of embittered but curious Czechs looked on in silence. The soldier in the turret sat huddled up against the driving snow, nervously fingering the trigger of his machine gun as he faced the crowd.' As Kennan later reported, for the rest of the day 'the motorized units pounded and roared over the cobblestone streets: hundreds and hundreds of vehicles plastered

German troops occupy the city while the stunned population looks on

German motorcycle troops at Prague Castle

German cavalry riding into Prague against the background of the Castle

Advance units of the German Army ask for directions from Prague policemen

German troops in the streets of Prague

with snow, the faces of the occupants red with what some thought was shame but what I fear was in most cases merely the cold.'

Blaskowitz established his headquarters at the Alcron Hotel and proclaimed a curfew beginning at 20:00. The only exemptions were doctors and railwaymen. Popular gatherings were forbidden. Actions hostile to the German Army would be punished under martial law. The red-bordered proclamation, translated into bad Czech and surmounted by the eagle and swastika, was plastered on walls throughout the city. Apart from a few scattered incidents of minor sabotage, in which the tyres of German lorries were slashed, there was no resistance. The crowds restricted themselves to wearing the Czech national colours in their buttonholes or hurling snowballs at passing military vehicles. The police cooperated with the new masters, controlling traffic and giving directions to troops lost in the tangled streets of the Old Town. German sentries with fixed bayonets

A German sentry on a street corner near Charles Bridge

appeared in front of all the hotels and public buildings. A correspondent from the London *Times* contrasted the appearance of these troops with the dejected khaki-clad soldiers of the Czech Army, helpless witnesses to the humiliation of their country.

While Blaskowitz was securing the Czech capital, Hitler made a sudden decision to visit his new conquest, taking a train to Česká Lípa in the Sudetenland. He was accompanied by the Reichsführer SS, Heinrich Himmler, and his deputy, Reinhard

German guards outside the Ambassador Hotel in Wenceslas Square

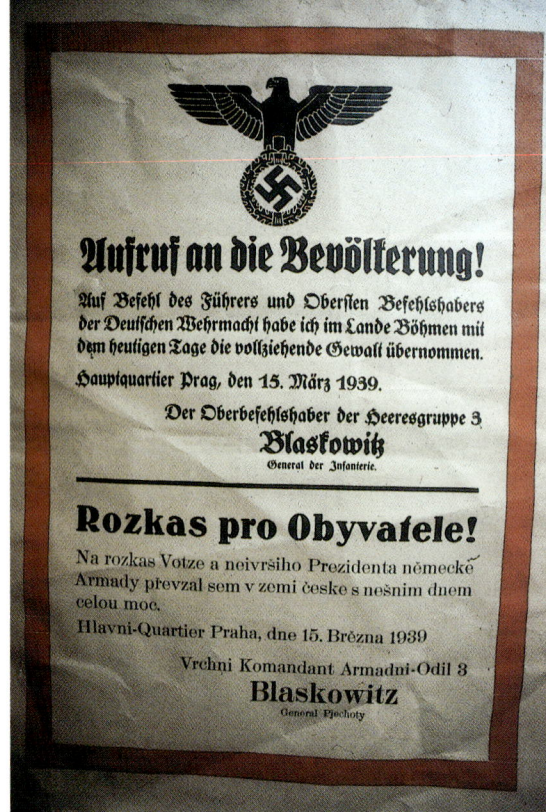

An announcement by the commander of the German occupation forces General Blaskowitz stating that by the order of the Führer he has assumed total power

Heydrich, the head of the Nazi security police, who were to play a sinister part in the future of the Czech lands. Other leading Nazi figures were also present, including Ribbentrop and Göring, fresh from their triumph over Hácha that morning. After a pause at Česká Lípa, perhaps to make sure that there was no fighting in the Czech capital, Hitler left for Prague by car, guided over the icy roads through the gathering dusk by SS Brigadeführer (Major-General) Karl Hermann Frank, a Sudeten German notorious for his hatred of the Czechs. The convoy had to force a way through snowdrifts and endless columns of troops and guns. Hitler entered Prague unseen by the Czechs, confined to their homes by the curfew, and reached Prague Castle just after 20:00. Security there had already been taken over by the élite SS troops of his personal bodyguard. Hitler arrived before Hácha whose train had been delayed in Berlin. When the State President finally reached the castle, he was forced to use the servants' entrance, a symbol of the new relationship between Czechs and Germans. In the future he would require the permission of the Nazi guard commander to enter or leave the presidential office.

From the upper windows of Prague Castle, Hitler gazed in triumph over the lights of the conquered city. Then he went downstairs to a special candlelit supper. Although a vegetarian and teetotaller, he nibbled Prague ham and drained a small glass of Pilsner beer, boasting to his entourage that Czechoslovakia had ceased to exist. Hitler spent the night in the castle guest rooms. Others were less comfortable. Frank slept on the floor of the Habsburger Salon with his knapsack for a pillow. But as he later recalled, it was the

happiest moment of his life – Bohemia-Moravia had been restored to the German Reich. While the Führer slept, officials worked on a document incorporating his pledge of Czech autonomy. By the morning of 16 March, the text was ready for Hitler's signature. A short statement containing thirteen articles, the decree proclaimed the 'Protectorate of Bohemia and Moravia.' German citizens of the former Czechoslovakia became citizens of the Reich. Czechs became nationals of the new Protectorate. They kept their own government, shorn of responsibility for defence, foreign affairs, communications and customs. They were subject to their own laws unless these conflicted with German laws. A Reichsprotektor, with his

A group of Nazi students cross Charles Bridge on their way to greet the Führer

Hitler arrives at the First Courtyard of Prague Castle

A Protectorate stamp based on the famous photograph of Hitler surveying his new conquest from a window of Prague Castle

Inside Prague Castle, Hitler prepares to sign the decree creating the Protectorate of Bohemia and Moravia, while Martin Bormann (extreme left) looks on

An enthusiastic German crowd salutes Hitler as he appears at a window of Prague Castle

seat in Prague, became Hitler's representative, guaranteeing that the Czech government acted in conformity with German interests. He could veto Czech legislation and dismiss Czech ministers. It was clear where real authority lay in this new system. The powers reserved to the Reichsprotektor ensured that Czech autonomy was subject to the whims of the Nazi masters in Berlin. The Czechs learned of their new status on the morning of 16 March when Ribbentrop broadcast the decree over Prague Radio and announced a new order in Central Europe. That evening Hácha made a speech defining independence as 'a short period in our national history' which had come to an end. The future lay in union with the Reich.

After signing the decree, Hitler lingered at Prague Castle. In the course of the morning he received the mayor of Prague, Dr Klapka, and the Czech Defences Minister, General Syrový. Around noon he appeared at a window overlooking the city and was greeted by cheers from a crowd of German soldiers and civilians waiting below. He then came down the stairs to the first courtyard to meet a group of students from the German University in Nazi uniforms who had marched to the castle across the ancient Charles Bridge carrying large swastika banners. Some were heavily bandaged, the supposed victims of Czech terrorism. His official photographer, Hoffman, was on hand to capture the scene. By early afternoon, Hitler

Hitler departs from Prague Castle

German sentries at the main entrance to Prague Castle

had evidently had enough of Prague and slipped away by car. It was the end of his first and only visit to the Czech capital. Before leaving, Hitler spoke to Frank and told him he would be wanted in the next few days. This ambiguous statement did not bode well for the Czechs. Two days later, at the Imperial Hotel in Vienna, Hitler appointed Baron Konstantin von Neurath to the new post of Reichsprotektor. A conservative German aristocrat, von Neurath had served as German Foreign Minister until February 1938 when he was replaced by Ribbentrop. Hitler's choice was dictated by the desire to install a respectable figurehead in Prague who still enjoyed some credibility abroad. His real purpose, however, was revealed in his choice of Neurath's deputy and German State Secretary, SS Brigadeführer Karl Hermann Frank, a rabid Nazi. As the London *Times* remarked, it was typical of Hitler to balance a moderate like Neurath with 'one of the worst . . . horsewhipping bullies of the upstart type,' a 'rancourous and vengeful' Sudeten 'determined to avenge upon the Czechs twenty years of subordination in the Republic between 1918 and 1938'.

The new system was not formally inaugurated until a month after the occupation. Between 15 March and 16 April 1939 the real power in Bohemia-Moravia was the German military. In Prague this meant the Third Army under General Blaskowitz, who acted with the advice of a civilian commissioner, Konrad Henlein, the Nazi Gauleiter (leader) of the Sudetenland and Frank's former boss. The existing Nazi organization in Bohemia was assigned to Henlein's Sudeten Gau and established its Prague headquarters on Kampa Island, near the Charles Bridge, in the former offices of the Prague Water Company. Blaskowitz does not seem to have relied much on Henlein who soon dropped into the background. Despite his unconcealed ambition, Henlein was never to play a prominent role in the politics of the Protectorate. In these early days, the troops were under strict orders to act correctly. On 4 April, Blaskowitz issued a proclamation announcing that the Germans came not as conquerors 'but in order to create the conditions for the peaceful collaboration of the peoples in this area'. His appeal was echoed by Professor Josef Pfitzner of the German University, installed as the deputy mayor of Prague. According to Pfitzner 'racial peace and joy' would reign between the nationalities 'on the banks of the Moldau'. As a symbol of goodwill Blaskowitz ordered an honour

guard on the tomb of the Unknown Soldier in Old Town Square and joined the former Czech Defence Minister, General Syrový, to lay wreaths there. German troops were required to salute when they passed the monument. It was noticeable, however, that the photograph of Masaryk, the founder of Czech independence, which had appeared on the tomb in the first days of the occupation, had been replaced by a huge swastika.

Down the highways to the German border thundered huge convoys of trailer trucks, up to forty vehicles at a time, loaded with looted stocks of steel, timber, textiles and food. Czechs grumbled as German soldiers thronged into shops to snap up goods unavailable in the Reich, food, textiles, crystal, shoes. There were bitter jokes about the apparently insatiable appetites of the occupying forces. As Kennan reported: 'The obvious enjoyment and astonishment with which the German officers and men set about to consume Bohemian food and to purchase Bohemian goods has created a deep impression on everyone who has witnessed it. With the mark made legal tender at a conversion rate of ten crowns to one mark, Prague shops and restaurants have done a thriving business ... people vie with each other in the repetition of tales of the gargantuan exploits of German officers and men in the local restaurants and beer halls.' In a paradoxical propaganda move, mobile kitchens from the Nazi welfare organization, Winterhilfe (Winter Help), moved in with the troops on 15 March to feed the Czechs who had supposedly been left to starve by their own government. Large wall posters informed passers-by that the poor and unemployed could receive a free hot lunch by registering at the local government offices. German journalists

A guidebook to Bohemia and Moravia for German soldiers

A Wehrmacht propaganda booklet for Czechs published in 1939 entitled German Soldiers – What everyone ought to know about the German armed forces

As a temporary measure Czech banknotes were overstamped 'Protectorate of Bohemia and Moravia'

A sign proclaiming that this is 'a purely Aryan shop'

claimed to have seen hope shining in the eyes of downtrodden Czechs who would now have 'work and bread . . . the birthright of every inhabitant of the Great German Reich.' Considerable ingenuity was devoted to securing pictures of Czech children pleading for food but the experiment was not a success and the canteens were soon withdrawn. In July 1939 the Protectorate government was suddenly presented with the bill for this welfare work. Czechs, it seemed, would have bear the costs of German propaganda.

Judengut in Überseekisten

Seit dem September vorigen Jahres hat sich in Prag viel geändert. So kann man nun die Abwanderung von Juden aus der Tschecho-Slowakei beobachten. Gleichzeitig legt jeder Arier Wert darauf, nicht für einen Juden gehalten zu werden

PRAG *heute*

"Židi ven!" — "Juden hinaus!"
kann man in den verschiedensten Stadtvierteln Prags lesen

Links:

Arbeitslager nach deutschem Vorbild

sollen den jugendlichen Arbeitslosen neuen Lebensinhalt geben. Noch beschränkt sich der Arbeitsdienst nur auf Arbeitslose, aber schon wurden Stimmen laut, die eine allgemeine Dienstpflicht forderten

Rechts:

"Tschechisch-arische Kanzlei"

schrieb z. B. ein Advokat unter sein Firmenschild, um nicht mit einem Juden verwechselt zu werden

A page from a Nazi propaganda magazine featuring anti-Semitic developments in Prague

In the early weeks of the occupation, Prague was spared the anti-Semitic outrages that had marked the Nazi seizure of Vienna the year before. Within days the first steps had been taken to 'Aryanize' Jewish firms and exclude Jews from the professions but there were no violent pogroms. For the time being, Hitler wanted to show a respectable face to the world. The Gestapo terror remained in the background. The arrival of the German Army was accompanied by a round-up of 5000 Jewish refugees, anti-Nazi journalists, and communists codenamed Aktion Gitter (Operation Fence) who were detained in a special camp at Milovice, near Prague. The arrests were made by Czech police, acting under the orders of the Gestapo, which had established its headquarters at the Palace Hotel on Panská Street. A few individuals escaped by hiding in cellars or abandoned houses. Others fled to the woods outside the city. But it was impossible to leave the Protectorate without a visa from the Gestapo and there was a new wave of suicides by those who despaired of the future. In one incident four Jews leapt one after the other from a high building in the centre of the city. Many Czech detainees were released from Milovice after pledging to abstain from politics. Anti-Nazi refugees, however, were deported to concentration camps in Germany.

The Czech army was disarmed and a guard placed over its arms dumps and military factories. The process of demobilization was supervised by General Friderici who later became the German military representative in the Protectorate. It was made an offence to conceal weapons from the Germans or to own a broadcasting set. Hácha was allowed to retain a small force of 7000 lightly armed men as a ceremonial guard but it was closely supervised. Press censorship intensified. This was enforced by Czechs although a Nazi chief censor, the former press attaché at

A small ceremonial guard was all that the Czech State President Emil Hácha was allowed to retain

A billboard announces the imminent change from left to right-hand drive imposed by the Germans - this came into effect on 26 March 1939, only eleven days after the occupation

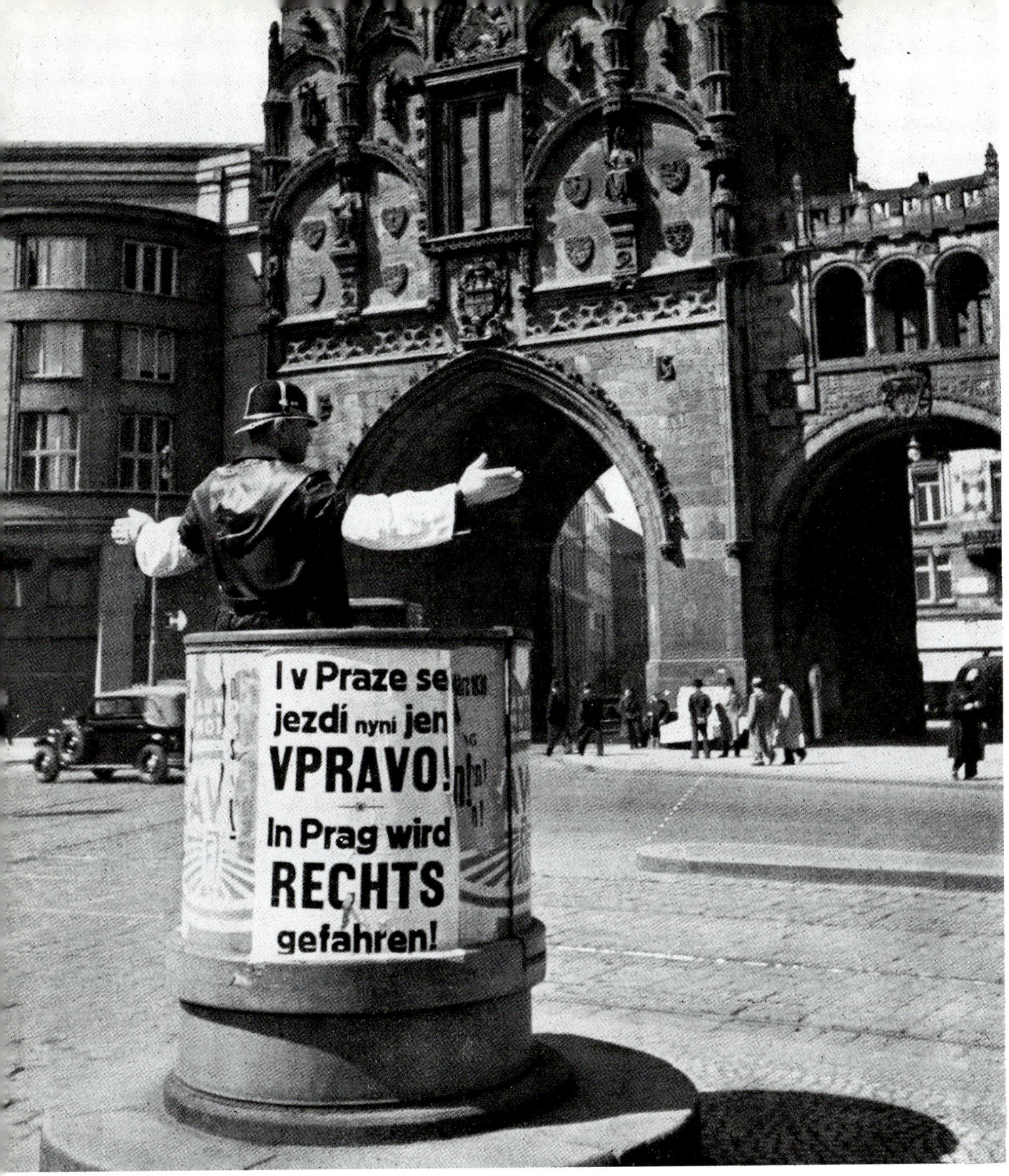

In front of the Powder Tower a Czech policemen supervises the new traffic system. The poster reads: 'Prague is now driving on the right'

A membership card for 'NS' - an organization which replaced the political parties under the Occupation

„VŠECHNY VÁS VOLÁM K VYTRVALOSTI.

Mnohými zkouškami ještě projdeme. Vědomí však, že jdeme společně a že všichni věříme ve šťastnou budoucnost své vlasti, nám dá sílu k další práci. Buďte si opravdu bratry a neopouštějte se ani v radosti ani v utrpení."

Dr. E. HÁCHA.

ČLENSKÝ PRŮKAZ

VLASTI ZDAR

NS

VÝBOR NÁRODNÍHO SOUručenství PRAHA SNĚMOVNA

generální tajemník

vedoucí Výboru N. S.

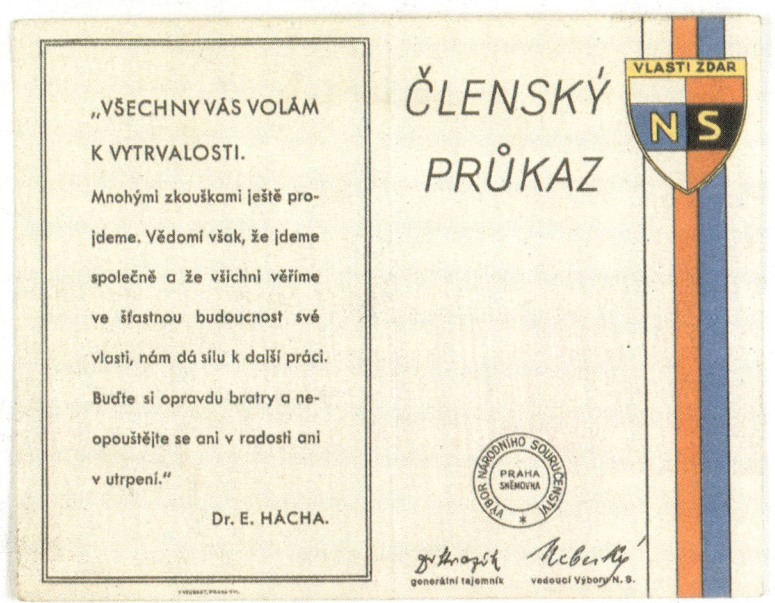

the German Embassy, von Gregory, held the ultimate authority. As early as 18 March the newspaper *A Zet* was closed down for publishing an unflattering portrait of Hitler. But few Czechs noticed much difference. The press had already been thoroughly muzzled before the occupation to avoid giving offence to Hitler's Germany. The most public change in this transitional period came on 26 March, when Czechs were ordered to drive on the right, or German, side of the road. The change had been debated for years under the old regime but was inaugurated overnight by the German Army. All over Prague Czech policemen enforced the regulation from traffic boxes displaying the new rules. Observing recent events from the American Legation, Kennan reported on 30 March that for the moment, the attitude of the new authorities had been 'surprisingly mild and conciliatory . . . I am encouraged to hope that their attitude toward the mass of the Czechs may turn out to be more hopeful than many had anticipated.'

Beneath Prague Castle a Czech policeman stands next to a poster proclaiming that the Nazi Welfare Organisation (NSV) will feed the starving

In the month after the occupation, the Czech government existed in limbo, awaiting the arrival of the Reichsprotektor. Hácha appeared an almost broken man. In this political vacuum the small extremist group, the National Fascist Community, under General Rudolf Gajda, modelled on Mussolini's Italy, made a bid for power in association with the equally unrepresentative neo-Nazi Vlajka (Flag) Party and the anti-Semitic ANO (Action for National Restoration), creating a Czech National Committee on 15 March and calling for wholehearted cooperation with the New Order. Although Gajda received limited support from the German military authorities in Prague, political turmoil did not suit the needs of Berlin which wanted peace and tranquillity in the Protectorate. Gajda found himself shunned by the occupiers and isolated when the Czech government, galvanized by his action, abolished the political parties and founded the National Solidarity (Národní Souručenství) Movement. Ostensibly a totalitarian move which eradicated the last vestiges of democracy, the new organization offered a defensive united front to the Germans. Worn upside down, the badge of the movement, a shield in the national colours with the initials NS, could be read to mean 'death to Germans' (Smrt Němcům). By May 1939 97.4 per cent of eligible Czechs had joined National Solidarity. At the end of May, a last attempt by the extreme right to gain power by fomenting riots, attacking Jews, and bombing cafés, was put down by Czech police while the Germans stood aside. The government was able safely to reject the demands of Gajda and his political allies. The incident confirmed Hitler's determination to rule through the established Czech authorities for the time being, a course that ensured German supremacy with the minimum of effort and expense.

By the time Gajda made his bid for power, Neurath had been installed as Reichsprotektor. He arrived at the main station in Prague on 5 April to receive a formal welcome from the commander of the German Army, General Brauchetsch, who had flown into Ruzyně earlier that morning. Bands played 'Deutschland Über Alles' and the 'Horst Wessel Song,' the anthem of the Nazi party, while a nineteen-gun salute crashed out over the city. No effort was spared to make the occasion a propaganda success. A national holiday was proclaimed and the Mayor of Prague appealed for a display of traditional Czech hospitality. Every German in the city turned out to greet Hitler's new viceroy and more were brought by special train from the Sudetenland. Householders were ordered to hang flags from their windows and each school and organization was told to send a delegation to line the official route. As

The new Reichsprotektor Baron Konstantin von Neurath arrives at Prague's main station on 5 April 1939

A German military parade in Wenceslas Square to mark von Neurath's arrival in the city

The new Reichsprotektor with President Hácha during the welcoming ceremony

Kennan, who witnessed the scene, reported, despite these extensive preparations, the day was not a success from the German point of view. Many householders preferred to pay a 600-crown fine rather than show a flag. Schoolchildren were kept at home by their parents or taken out for a day in the country. The crowds were sparse, with only the Germans and a few Czech fascists showing any enthusiasm as Neurath passed by: 'The same situation repeated itself later when the Reichsprotektor, still accompanied by his motorized guard of honor, proceeded to and from Wenceslas Square for the military parade. The sidewalks of the square were crowded throughout the parade, but no

A sign on Narodni Street adverising the White Horse - a German beer cellar offering music, dancing and 'good cheer'

more than on any fine holiday morning; and a good half of the people preferred to stroll along in their wonted fashion rather than join those who thronged the curb. The torchlight tattoo at night attracted no more than three or four hundred people, out of a city of a million, and most of those who attended were Germans.' At the same time the parade was a potent show of military force, with tanks and heavy guns grinding through the streets while bombers droned through the sky above the National Museum.

Neurath tried to reassure the Czechs, echoing the conciliatory line pursued by Blaskowitz. In his first speech he pledged to lead Bohemia-Moravia to 'happiness and prosperity.' According to Neurath he had 'no greater wish than that the Czech people should recognize our mission and their own, and should help me to fulfil my difficult task to the best of their ability by honest collaboration.' The Czech government was reorganized. Hácha remained State President and General Alois Eliáš became the new premier. As military adviser to the Czechoslovak government in the early thirties, Eliáš had attended disarmament conferences in Geneva where he first met Neurath. Now it was said that they chatted together in French, the traditional language of diplomacy. In presenting his government to the Reichsprotektor, Eliáš acknowledged that the tasks of the future could mean life or death for the Czech people. Despite this public commitment to mutual collaboration there was tension beneath the surface. Sir Paul Dukes, who had been a British secret agent in Russia during the Bolshevik revolution, visited the city at this time to find a missing refugee. He had been asked to undertake this task because his reputation as a ferocious anti-Communist provided some protection in dealing with the Gestapo. Dukes found the atmosphere in Prague full of menace: 'On the surface people carried on their existence as before, plied their trades, enjoyed their amusements. At eight in the morning the shops were already open, the cafés serving early customers. Numerous booths displayed an array of newspapers in many tongues. But this was all superficial. The black-uniformed SS guards striding along in pairs, the high-powered cars with huge swastika flags painted on them (so that they couldn't be torn off), carrying batches of German officers and soldiers hither and thither, were constant reminders that the city no longer belonged to its inhabitants. Very necessary to the invaders were these precautions. For beneath the surface the fire of revolt smouldered defiantly. Two months 'protection' had only served finally to exacerbate the populace.'

Czechs showed their opposition to the Nazi New Order by displays of passive resistance. Hitler's birthday on 20 April was ignored by the people of Prague who chose instead to lay bunches of flowers on the Jan Hus statue in Old Town Square. The centrepiece was a wreath over a yard high emblazoned with

the national motto, Pravda Vítězí (Truth Shall Prevail). In the afternoon Czech police removed this provocative symbol but it was replaced by a chalice, the symbol of the medieval Hussites, who were widely regarded as the first Czech nationalists. On 5 May flowers were laid on the monument to the US President Woodrow Wilson outside the main station. Wilson's commitment to national self-determination during the First World War had helped to create an independent Czechoslovak state. The reburial of the nineteenth-century poet Karel Mácha, whose remains were transferred from the Sudetenland to Prague on 6 May, produced another demonstration of national feeling that brought out more flags than on any holiday ordered by the Germans. These events were monitored by Kennan who reported on 11 May 'a recent scene at the National Theater where the Prague Orchestra's rendition of Smetana's patriotic suite, *Má Vlast* (My Country), was followed by a wild ovation which lasted for a full quarter of an hour and which ended with the conductor kissing the score and holding it up before the audience.' The Germans later banned the piece because of its nationalist sentiments.

The population displayed a Švejk-like ability for procrastination and passive resistance. As the US Consul General in Prague reported on 17 July, people in cinemas made 'wisecracks, under cover of the darkness, over the German newsreels. Czech waiters in the cafés infuriate their German patrons by always handing them the *Vöelkischer Beobachter* (The Nazi Party newspaper) face down. Germans sometimes find their parked cars decorated with the hammer and sickle, and the old ČSR licence tags (Czechoslovak Republic) changed to read USSR).' At the beginning of June, Pfitzner, the Nazi Deputy Mayor of Prague, complained that orders for the erection of German street signs had been ignored. Moreover the population was insulting its new masters by replying, 'I don't understand (Nerozumím),' to every statement in German, an intolerable situation in a city that was now part of the Reich. According to the leader of the German Nazi Party in Prague, Karl Hoess, Bohemia remained an area of struggle between

A sign in a Prague pub asking the customers to 'kindly refrain from discussing politics'

The Nazis imposed bilingual street signs throughout the city

the nationalities. On 11 July Frank issued a decree ordering the use of German and Czech on all official correspondence. The German language was to appear first and was to take legal precedence in the event of a disputed translation. Certain words including 'Führer' and 'Reichsprotektor' could appear only in their German form. On 18 July the newspaper *Národní Listy* was suspended for three days when it responded with an article entitled 'Speak Czech,' arguing that 'the purity of the language' was 'the foundation of the National Spirit.' The US Consul General concluded that such incidents showed Czechs and Germans were still on different roads 'and nothing serious is being done to bring them together.'

clearly that speculations about a rapid end of the situation created in Central Europe by the Führer are false. Where once the swastika flies, there it will fly forever. The German Reich is not Austria-Hungary and 1918 will not come again.' The Germans knew who was behind the agitation in the Protectorate and would strike when the time was ripe. Three days later, on 8 June, Frank turned his words into deeds after a German policeman was shot dead in Kladno. Without waiting for an investigation or a post-mortem, he ordered the arrest of the council and several prominent citizens. The community was accused of harbouring a paid assassin in the service of Beneš and forced to pay a collective fine of 500,000 crowns. The hostages

The SS guard battalion marching across Charles Bridge

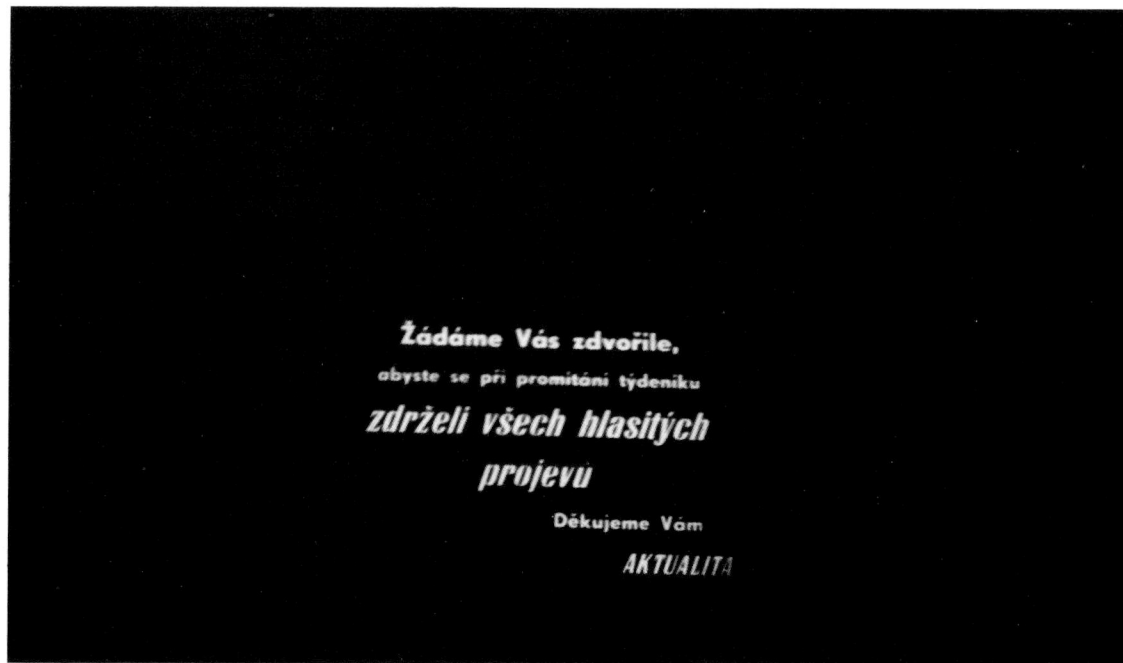

An announcement on a Prague cinema screen: 'We kindly request the audience to refrain from loud comments during the newsreel. Thank you'

As Europe slid towards war over Poland in the summer of 1939, the German attitude hardened. On 27 June the Reichsprotektor was given increased powers which allowed him to make laws himself in an emergency or to modify laws passed by the Czech government. Such laws immediately became part of the Czech penal code without the necessity of confirmation by the courts. The population was repeatedly warned against any attempt at rebellion or collusion with the exile movement abroad which had begun to form around former President Edvard Beneš. In a speech at Budějovice on 5 June, Frank stated that Czechs could share 'in the blessings and benefits of the Reich. But there can be no peace with those people who think they can cheat us with the old Beneš methods, people who either openly or secretly are still ogling Dr Beneš. It must be said

were badly beaten by the Gestapo and the mayor was thrown to his death from a fourth-floor window of the Špilberk Fortress in Brno.

This heavy-handed display was reinforced by Henlein on 27 June in a speech to the Nazi party in Prague, pledging that rebellion would be severely punished. In the event of trouble the Reich would not hesitate to respond with brutal force. An avalanche of new orders and restrictions descended on the Czechs. It was made an offence to whistle or boo during German newsreel films. Offending audiences were expelled without refunds and the cinema closed for eight days. Teachers who failed to collaborate or who encouraged their pupils in nationalist displays were dismissed. The singing of patriotic songs in pubs and cafés was banned.

It became an offence to wear the national colours in buttonholes. The death sentence was introduced for concealing arms or cutting German military telephone wires. At the end of August the Czechoslovak Legion, a veterans organization for soldiers who had joined the independence movement during the First World War, was dissolved. Its property in Prague was handed over to the SS. It became an act of treason, punishable by death, to join the exile movement abroad. Within days of the outbreak of war in September, secret orders were issued to the German Army that any exiles caught in foreign uniform were to be murdered on their way to prisoner of war camps. Jewish soldiers were to be handed over to the Gestapo.

As the Polish crisis deepened in August 1939, both sides were biding their time. To keep the Czechs quiet and appease foreign opinion, Hitler allowed the respectable face of the occupation, von Neurath, to set the pace. But in the background lurked SS Brigadeführer Karl Hermann Frank, the German State Secretary. As Höhere SS und Polizei Führer (Higher SS and Police Leader – HSSPF), Frank controlled the security police and was answerable not to von Neurath but to Himmler and Heydrich in Berlin. Through his police apparatus, the SS leadership could shape events in the Protectorate without and, if necessary, against the Reichsprotektor. As for the Czechs, they regarded the occupation as temporary. They hoped that Hitler's demands on Poland would finally force Britain, France, and perhaps Russia, into war with Germany and spell the end of the Nazi system. The Nazi-Soviet pact of August 1939 was discounted. Whispered propaganda stated that Stalin had only signed this agreement on condition that Czechoslovakia was restored within its 1938 borders. Beneš would return to Prague in triumph on 28 October, Czechoslovak National Day. After five months of occupation, the Czechs were disarmed but by no means demoralized. As early as 14 April, Kennan reported: 'There is probably no country in Europe where war – and war at the earliest possible date – is so universally desired as in the Protectorate of Bohemia and Moravia . . . In the event of an unsuccessful war at any time during the next few years, the Germans will probably find that the Czech spirit of independence, despite the subjection of the people to all the propaganda methods of the modern totalitarian state, has shown surprising powers of endurance.' This indeed was the eventual outcome but it was to take longer than anyone in Prague had believed possible as spring turned to summer in the fateful year of 1939.

'I have fallen totally in love with this city.
It exudes the German spirit and must
become German again one day'

JOSEPH GOEBBELS, 7 NOVEMBER 1940

CHAPTER TWO

The New Masters

The Reichsprotektor's standard on the roof of Prague Castle with the Czech presidential flag in the background

A commemorative sheet of stamps featuring Prague Castle with a swastika flag and the flag of the Protectorate

ON 3 SEPTEMBER 1939, two days after Hitler invaded Poland, Britain and France declared war on Germany. The Czechs hoped for the speedy collapse of the Nazi system but they were to be disappointed. Poland was crushed by a lightning campaign while its western allies remained on the defensive. Stalin signed the Nazi-Soviet pact with Hitler and joined in the destruction of the Polish state. Behind the victorious German armies, Himmler's SS squads launched a ruthless campaign of murder and forced resettlement against the Polish people. In the Protectorate, Nazi propaganda emphasized that the Czechs had avoided similar destruction only by accepting subordination to the Reich. The implications were obvious. If the Czechs made trouble, they would lose their unique status in the Nazi New Order and share the fate of the Poles. As the German press emphasized, the defeat of Poland had dispelled Czech illusions of liberation and underlined the wisdom of collaboration by displaying the iron fist of the Reich. According to Frank, the Czechs had Hitler to thank for the fact that their towns and cities were not in ruins and the blood of thousands of young Czechs had not been spilled.

On the eve of war, the Germans took precautions against unrest in the Protectorate. The powers of the Frank's security police were expanded and there was a wave of pre-emptive arrests, Operation Albrecht, against the individuals considered most likely to cause trouble. Nearly 2000 were detained and sent to the concentration camps at Dachau and Buchenwald as hostages for Czech good behaviour. Despite these repressive measures a number of resistance groups continued to survive. In the wake of the Nazi occupation, former Czech officers founded the Obrana národa (National Defence) as the framework of an underground army. Politically the ON was the most right-wing of the resistance organizations. In the middle was the Politické ústředí (Political Centre) which established links with the National Solidarity organization and the Protectorate regime. On the left was the Petiční výbor 'Věrni zůstaneme' (Committee of the Petition 'We Remain Faithful'). The PVVZ attracted trade unionists and former members of the Social Democratic Party. In early 1940 these organizations formed a Central Committee of the Home Resistance (ÚVOD) in Prague which acknowledged the leadership of the exiles in London under Edvard Beneš. The Communist Party of Czechoslovakia (CPC), which had previously taken a strong nationalist stance, was confused by the Nazi-Soviet Pact and the new line from Moscow condemning the war as an imperialist struggle of no interest to the working class. Communist publications

An SA unit marching across Charles Bridge

claimed that an allied victory would merely transfer the Czechs from one form of capitalist tyranny to another and accused Beneš of acting as the tool of British colonialism. The Gestapo harried the Communists less than other resistance groups because their rhetoric kept the Czechs divided and gave credibility to German propaganda about British plutocracy: 'A Nazi paid hireling could not have done it nearly so well.'

The crushing German victory in Poland made plans for an early uprising unrealistic. At the same time the resistance looked for other ways of embarrassing the Germans and raising national morale. A rumour was spread that the Saturday takings of the Prague tramway company were to be donated to the Nazi Winterhilfe (Winter Help) fund. The Czechs called such whispered propaganda 'JPP' campaigns after the initials of the phrase 'A woman told me.' On 30 September tram stops were picketed throughout the city and people walked, even from the distant suburbs. The Germans took no action but tried to claim that Czechs were protesting at the delay in banning Jews from the trams. The successful transport boycott was merely the preliminary to a much bigger demonstration on Czechoslovak National Day, 28 October, the first under occupation. Leaflets began to circulate in Prague calling for a peaceful demonstration. Czechs were told to avoid provoking the Germans by insults or violence. They were to come into the city wearing their best clothes with the national colours in their buttonholes. They were to boycott the Nazi-controlled press and the trams with their destination boards in Czech and German, symbols of the hated occupation. The day was to end with two minutes silence at the top of Wenceslas Square. The Communists, who had still not fully absorbed the new line from Moscow, went further, calling for a general strike and a demonstration of solidarity in front of the Soviet consulate. These plans were known both to the Protectorate government and to the Germans. On 23 October the Minister of the Interior, Josef Ježek, approached the Nazi security police commander, Walther Stahlecker, and asked that the Czech police should be allowed to control the situation. Stahlecker, however, gave no firm commitment. As for Neurath, he arranged to leave Prague, either because he did not believe that there would be real trouble or did not want to become involved in the kind of repressive measures necessary to put it down.

Saturday, 28 October, began quietly. There were few work stoppages, but most of the population went out wearing the national colours or 'Masaryk' caps, of the kind popularized by the father of Czechoslovak independence. By 11:00 large numbers had gathered in Wenceslas and Old Town Squares. There the first trouble began. Groups of German students wearing swastikas began tearing the national colours from the buttonholes of passersby or knocking off their caps. It had the appearance of a planned provocation. A series of running fights broke out. At the Petschek Palace on Bredauergasse, headquarters of the Prague Gestapo, a large crowd gathered to shout slogans against the occupation. As the situation deteriorated, Stahlecker telephoned Ježek, the Czech Interior Minister, to say that the SS guard battalion, Leibstandarte Adolf Hitler, under Obergruppenführer (General) Sepp Dietrich, intended to hold its usual Saturday parade through Wenceslas

German troops in the heart of Prague

Charles Bridge in the early months of the occupation

Square. If the Czechs could not control the situation, the SS would act. Faced with the threat of indiscriminate bloodshed, Czech police cleared the area and the SS parade went off without incident. But by 15:00 Wenceslas Square was again full of demonstrators, fighting with German civilians and off-duty SS men. German notices were destroyed and destination boards ripped from trams. The entrance to the Palace Hotel, the living quarters of the Prague Gestapo, was blocked by angry Czechs chanting: 'The bloodhounds live here.' Around the Wenceslas Statue in front of the National Museum, others shouted slogans in favour of Beneš or Stalin while the Czech police stood by. Demonstrations also occurred in Charles Square and at the main railway station.

At 16:00 Frank demanded a meeting with Hácha who was spending the weekend at his summer residence in Lány, outside Prague. Hácha summoned Eliáš and Ježek to join him. An hour later Frank turned up with Stahlecker in tow. The Germans warned the Czech ministers that unless order was restored, they would unleash the SS on the city. In the face of this threat, the Czech police finally acted and began clearing Wenceslas Square at 18:00. The day might have ended peacefully but for the arrival of armed German police detachments (Ordnungspolizei), ordered into the streets by Frank, which opened fire indiscriminately on groups of demonstrators. Frank himself was seen on the steps of the National Museum with a whip in his hand, directing operations. By the time peace had been restored, one Czech was dead and fifteen badly wounded. Several hundred more were injured but did not report to hospitals lest they attracted the unwelcome attention of the Gestapo. Of 400 arrested only fifty were taken into custody by the Czech police who had shown their sympathy with the demonstrators throughout the day. The city centre was littered with torn German posters and the smashed destination boards from 175 trams. The following morning, Sunday 29 October, tension remained high. The Czech government suspended the tram service and issued appeals over the radio and street loudspeakers for Czechs to stop wearing the national colours and Masaryk caps. Only the badge of National Solidarity was permitted. Once again, however, there were incidents when small groups of Germans tried to tear NS badges from Czech lapels. Real trouble was only prevented by the prompt action of the Czech police and the day ended without major incidents.

The whole confrontation had undoubtedly

The Czernin Palace housed the German bureaucracy under the State Secretary Karl Hermann Frank who became the most powerful figure in the Protectorate

been engineered by Frank and his SS masters in Berlin who hoped for total power in the Protectorate. By provoking trouble on the streets of Prague, they hoped to rouse Hitler's anger against the Czechs and dispense with Neurath, the moderate face of the occupation. On 30 October, Frank was promoted to the rank of SS Gruppenführer (Lieutenant General), a sure sign that Himmler approved of his actions. In Berlin the Nazi Propaganda Minister, Joseph Goebbels, noted in his diary: 'The demonstrations in Prague were . . . quite widespread. Shots were fired, one death and a number seriously injured. Things were allowed to go too far. Neurath does not take enough precautions.' But at first it seemed that the conspiracy had failed to produce the required results. The German news media suppressed reports of the demonstrations which contradicted the official propaganda line about peace and order in the Protectorate. Hácha blamed German provocation and Neurath seemed to agree. Returning to Prague on 31 October, the Reichsprotektor expressed his regret that he had been away and criticized Frank's actions during his absence. Neurath promised that all those arrested would be speedily released without charge. The Czech regime, which was well aware of the rivalry within the Nazi administration, concluded that in the struggle with Frank, Neurath had won the first round. The SS, however, was merely biding its time.

During the firing on 28 October, a young Czech medical student, Jan Opletal, was fatally wounded by a German bullet. He died in hospital on 11 November. The Prague students regarded Opletal as a martyr and requested permission to hold a funeral procession through the streets. The Nazi security police granted permission for the procession but banned the students from attending the burial. After the Protectorate government had obtained a pledge from the student leaders that there would be no anti-German demonstrations, the Gestapo withdrew even this restriction. The Czech police and the student organizers were made responsible for the maintenance of order and leaflets were issued calling for a peaceful demonstration. It is clear, however, that Frank was hoping for trouble which would justify radical action. Nor could Neurath stop him. Contradicting his words to Hácha, the Reichsprotektor had endorsed Frank's account of events on 28 October in a report to Berlin. Indeed he had pledged that any further disorder would be ruthlessly suppressed by the SS guard battalion. This was probably an attempt to appear tough, but

K. H. Frank and W. Frick with President Hácha

it limited his freedom of action and played into the hands of his SS rivals.

On the evening of 14 November, a wake was held for Opletal at U Fleků, a Prague pub popular with students. The following morning over 3000 filed past the coffin which lay in state at the Institute of Pathology. A long procession then set off down Alberthof Street into Hamenov. As the column approached Charles Square some of the students began to sing the National Anthem and other patriotic songs. At this point the Czech police, who were out in force, broke up the demonstration. The crowd dispersed into smaller groups. Some gathered in the nearby Charles Square where they shouted nationalist slogans. Others escaped through the Prague Technical University on Ressel Street and marched along the embankment tearing down German street signs and tram destination boards which they threw into the river. At Smetana Bridge, one group went up Victoria Street into Wenceslas Square. Another 150 continued along the embankment to the Mendel Bridge where they occupied the Law Faculty of Charles University. The building was cleared by troops of the SS guard battalion and three students were injured. Elsewhere in the city fights broke out between students and groups of Germans armed with rubber truncheons. One of the incidents involved Frank's SS driver who was supposedly wounded. Despite these

Jan Opletal, whose funeral sparked off student demonstrations

A poster dated 17 November 1939 announcing the closing of Czech universities and draconian anti-student measures

outbreaks, there was far less trouble than on 28 October and the citizens of Prague did not join in the demonstration.

Frank, however, had the evidence he wanted. On 16 November he flew to Berlin, accompanied by Neurath and the German military representative, General Friderici. Hitler, who had narrowly escaped an assassination attempt in Munich only a week before, was in an angry mood. He raged against the Czechs, regretting that he had not subjected them to the same treatment as the Poles. If there were any further manifestations of resistance, he would not hesitate to evacuate every German from Prague and level the city to the ground with heavy artillery. Meanwhile he ordered reprisals against the students and the closure of all institutions of higher learning for three years. This was intended to strike a blow at the intelligentsia, whom Hitler identified with the hated Czech 'national idea.' His words were music to Frank's ears. As for Neurath, he did not dare to contradict the SS version of events. Frank hurried back to Prague on the official plane, leaving Neurath behind to take the train. Once again the Reichsprotektor wanted to avoid implication in the bloody business of repression. Frank went straight from Ruzyně Airport to the Petschek Palace for a meeting with his security chiefs. There he ordered the arrest and execution of the student leaders and police raids on student halls of residence throughout Prague. The speed with which the operation was mounted suggests that the preparations had already been made.

At 23:30 the nine leaders of the student union were arrested during a committee meeting, driven to the SS barracks at Prague-Ruzyně and shot without trial. None had a record of resistance and one was deputy chairman of the 'Union for Cooperation with the Germans', a collaborationist front. Before dawn the following morning, 17 November, German security police and SS troops broke into halls of residence throughout Prague. Some students were shot as they jumped out of windows in an attempt to escape. Others attempted to resist behind makeshift barricades before being overwhelmed. In the women's dormitories there were many cases of rape and sexual assault. The prisoners were tied in twos and herded on to a fleet of city buses under a hail of blows and kicks from their SS guards. They were driven to Ruzyně where foreigners and Czech collaborators were released. The remainder, around 1,200, were subjected to further assaults by the SS. That afternoon they were taken to Oranienburg concentration camp outside Berlin, where they were held as hostages for Czech good behaviour. During the journey they were allowed neither food nor drink. Czech villagers who attempted to pass bread and water through the windows when the convoy halted, were savagely beaten with rifle butts. In the aftermath of the raids, the people of Prague remarked bitterly that Hitler had killed more 'protected' Czechs than 'enemy' Frenchmen since the beginning of the war.

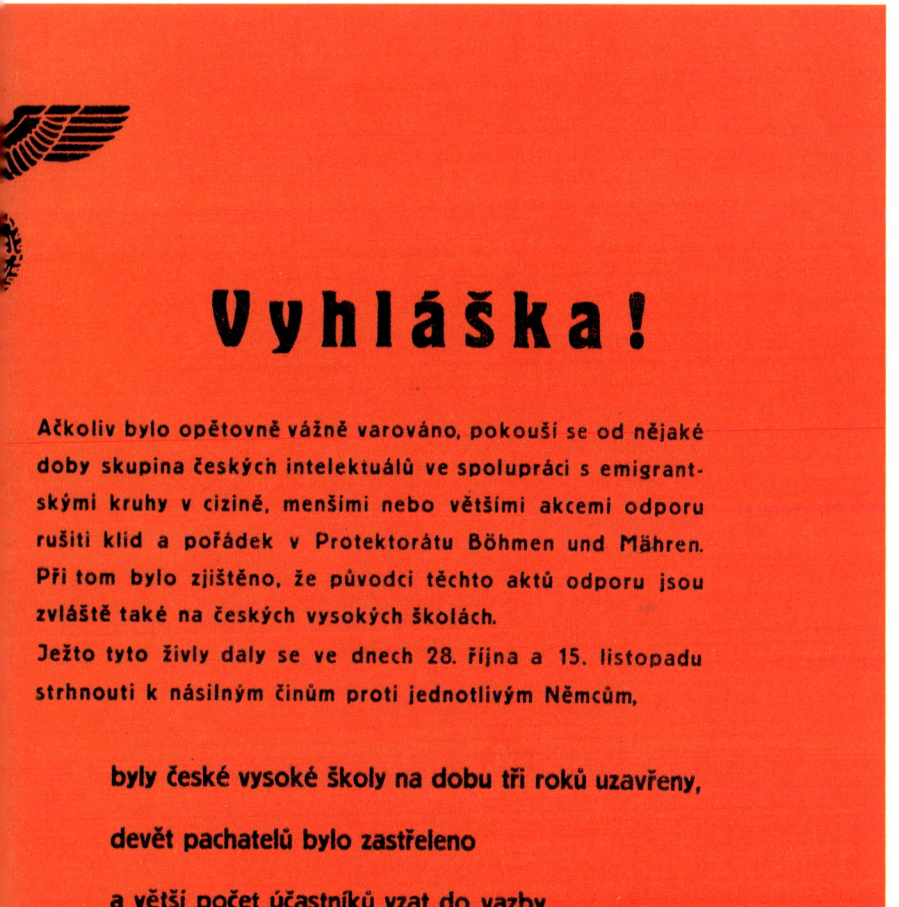

The empty academies in Prague were taken over by the German University or by the SS. Irreplaceable libraries and scientific collections were vandalized or dispersed. There were protest meetings in the Balkans which had traditionally sent many students to Charles University, the oldest in Central Europe. Prague itself, however, was like a dead city, the silent streets patrolled by German police in full battle gear with fingers on the triggers of their guns. On 21 November, as a show of force, the SS paraded through Wenceslas Square with bands and banners. Obeying a new decree published the previous day, Czech passersby had to stand to attention and take off their hats as a sign of respect for the swastika, the German National Anthem and the 'Horst Wessel Song'. Hitler's Propaganda Minister, Josef Goebbels, noted with satisfaction that the SS had created 'a deep impression. Prague is paralysed, silent with awe'. Neurath washed his hands of these outrages and retired for a time to his estates in Germany. On 2 December 1939, Frank warned that the Reich would not tolerate further acts of resistance: 'Whoever is not with us is against us, and whoever is against us will be ground to pieces.'

The closure of the universities and the arrest of the students was the first move in an attempt to split the Czechs by persecuting intellectuals and the well educated, regarded by the Nazis as irreconcilable supporters of the 'national idea', while cultivating the working class, whose labour was useful to Germany. According to Hitler, 'the Prague intelligentsia must be disarmed'. The Nazis boasted that war orders had soaked up unemployment and improved living conditions. There was some truth to this claim. Between March and June 1939, unemployment fell from 93,000 to under 17,000. By August 80,000 Czech workers had been lured to the Reich by the shortage of skilled labour there and the prospect of better wages. When rationing was imposed on the Protectorate in October 1939, it was on a more generous scale than in Germany. As Goebbels remarked, the Czech people wanted 'to live and to eat'. But the Nazis were not motivated by any spirit of goodwill towards Czech workers. The aim was to destroy national consciousness by a spurious appeal to social justice, paving the way for ultimate Germanization, while securing valuable labour for the German war effort. As Hitler himself remarked, the Protectorate armaments industry was 'extremely efficient. The Czechs

possess a natural gift for technical matters.'

Despite Frank's triumph in November 1939, his period of unchallenged authority proved merely temporary. Hitler was not yet prepared to hand total power over the Czechs to the SS. He wanted to keep that threat in reserve. Neurath was soon back at the Hradčany, mouthing the old rhetoric about peace and cooperation. In a New Year message to the Czech people he looked forward to an undisturbed, healthy and ever-closer relationship between Bohemia/Moravia and the Reich. Hitler too showed that he could whisper as well as shout. In an exchange of messages with Hácha on 15 March 1940, the first anniversary of the occupation, he denied any intention of threatening the national existence of the Czechs whom he hoped to save from the ravages of war. As a special reward the Protectorate guard was allowed to join the military parade held to mark the occasion and Hácha appeared on the reviewing stand. But for the Czechs everything had changed. As Hitler intended, they now understood that the Nazis would stop at nothing. Prague was swept by a wave of terrifying rumours that hospitals were forcibly sterilizing Czech women and giving children deadly injections.

In the aftermath of the Gestapo terror, Czech officials were threatened for any display of nationalist sentiment. The Mayor of Prague, Dr Otakar Klapka, laid a wreath on the tomb of the unknown soldier on

The proclamation of martial law in the wake of the student disturbances in November 1939

23 December 1939. Two weeks later he did the same at the statue of a former Mayor of Prague. Klapka argued that he had acted as a private individual, an excuse dismissed by his Nazi deputy, Professor Pfitzner. According to Pfitzner, Prague was a German city and displays of sympathy with the former regime by municipal officials were intolerable. Something would have to be done about ideological attitudes at the town hall. In July 1940, Klapka was arrested for supporting 'an illegal group inimical to the state and entertaining treasonable relations abroad'. He was executed the following year. Real power was vested in Pfitzner and German bureaucrats dominated the city administration. In February 1940, Frank's security police rounded up hundreds of members of the Czech gymnastic organization, SOKOL, a traditional bastion of nationalism, in an attempt to weaken every possible source of organized opposition.

As the Nazi grip tightened, the national mood was grim. Hatred of the occupation was combined with a sense of powerlessness. Many responded with symbolic actions like boycotting German films and art exhibitions. In February 1940 sporting contests between Czechs and Germans were banned because spectators were using the anonymity of the crowd to hiss and boo at the German side. The first anniversary of the occupation in March 1940 was marked by empty streets and a dearth of flags. Czechs failed to contribute to a German metal collection for war industry and stayed away from Hitler's birthday parade in Prague on 20 April. The renaming of Prague streets provided an opportunity for anti-Nazi jokes. It was suggested that Hrdlořezy (Cutthroats) should be called Es kommt der Tag (The day will come) and Klamovka (Mystification), named after the DNB, the official Nazi news agency. But these gestures had little effect on the reality of German power. An anonymous Czech wrote of the period: 'Foreign occupation changes every detail of one's whole life – not only public life, but ordinary, daily private life... Everything you look at has the hand of occupation upon it. You are ordered about by notices in the street... Every time you pass these inscriptions you are forced to realize afresh that you are no longer master in your own country... The changes penetrate every detail of your daily life. You must see the names in your village written up in German, hear the names of the tram stops shouted out in German. If you turn on the radio or open a paper, you are shouted at and stared at by insults and outrages... The whole atmosphere is somehow unhealthy and all the details of normal life become abnormal. You are under a permanent pathological tension... You cannot get rid of it and you cannot wash it off... I am sure that our people are longing not only to be free of the Germans but to have a normal sane life again, like normal human beings. Now they live in a sort of organized madness... I wonder if we shall all go mad with freedom and happiness when the war is over, or whether we will be too tired.'

There was another side to passive resistance, collaboration, which grew in response to German pressure on the population. Vlajka (Flag), an extremist party on the Nazi model, remained small and unrepresentative as were various openly anti-Semitic groups, but there were plenty of opportunists ready to claim German origins and change the spelling of their names. These people rose to positions of petty power as journalists, foremen in the factories, interpreters for the Gestapo and dealers in Black Market goods secured by contacts with corrupt Nazi officials. Then there were the secret collaborators, the army of Czech informers which underpinned German rule. Few adopted this role from conviction. Some were blackmailed by threats to their families, others were trying to insure themselves against becoming victims of the SS terror. Many used anonymous denunciations as way of paying off old scores against friends, neighbours, even members of their own family. The Gestapo was never short of accusations against people accused of listening to allied radio broadcasts, making jokes about Hitler or hoarding rationed food,

By order, a notice was attached to every radio set warning that listening to foreign broadcasts was punishable by death

The Old Town Hall

A Hitler Youth parade outside Czernin Palace

apparently petty offences which, however, could carry the death sentence under the Nazis. The existence of this secret army was encouraged by the Gestapo which had perfected its skill at exploiting the worst in human nature during the early years of Hitler's dictatorship. Fear of informers divided neighbour from neighbour and undermined the bonds of civil society. People were encouraged to avoid trouble and mind their own business, never knowing when the blow might fall.

The only hope for the Czechs lay in the defeat of Germany but on the battlefronts the news became worse instead of better. In April 1940, Hitler invaded Denmark and Norway. In May the German blitzkrieg was launched against France and the Low Countries. By June France had surrendered and Hitler stood triumphant on the shores of the English Channel. In the euphoria of victory there were demands for radical action in Bohemia/Moravia. The Gauleiter of the Sudetenland, Konrad Henlein, and of the

A group of German soldiers on the corner of Old Town Square

Lower Danube, Hugo Jury, wanted to abolish the Protectorate and integrate Bohemia/Moravia into the Reich. This would have allowed Henlein to establish his headquarters in Prague and Jury to move into Brno, away from the dreary provincial towns which they presently occupied. In a rare moment of unity, however, this solution was opposed by both Neurath and Frank who argued that only through the Protectorate could the Reich maintain a unified approach to the Czechs and pave the way for ultimate Germanization. In September 1940, Hitler agreed to maintain the Protectorate for the duration of the war. In the meantime the first steps were to be taken towards 'prospective Germanization of the area and its inhabitants'. While the majority of the population might ultimately qualify for assimilation, those 'about whom there exist doubts from a racial point of view or who are antagonistic towards the Reich should be excluded . . . This category should be exterminated.' The decision represented a triumph for the SS,

Winterhilfe (Winter Help) rally in the Old Town Square to appeal for warm clothing for the German soldiers fighting in Russia

which was in charge of Nazi racial policy. In October 1940 Himmler ordered the head of the German Security Police, Reinhard Heydrich, to start identifying possible candidates for Germanization, using school medical reports and old conscription records. It suited Hitler to avoid radical action on the Polish model. Even in this moment of victory, his thoughts were already turning towards the conquest of Russia in which the Czech railway network and arms industry would play an important role. While he distrusted the Czechs, he admired their technical ability and was unwilling to drive them to desperation if it could be avoided. As Goebbels noted in May 1941: 'The Führer has great praise for the work the Czechs have been doing in the armaments field. Not a single case of sabotage to date. And what they produce is good, serviceable and solid . . . They are hard-working and reliable. A valuable acquisition for us.' The Protectorate regime did everything possible to appease Hitler, pledging unity with the Reich and

A Hitler Youth parade in Wenceslas Square

A clandestine photo of SS bandsmen at lunch in an outdoor restaurant

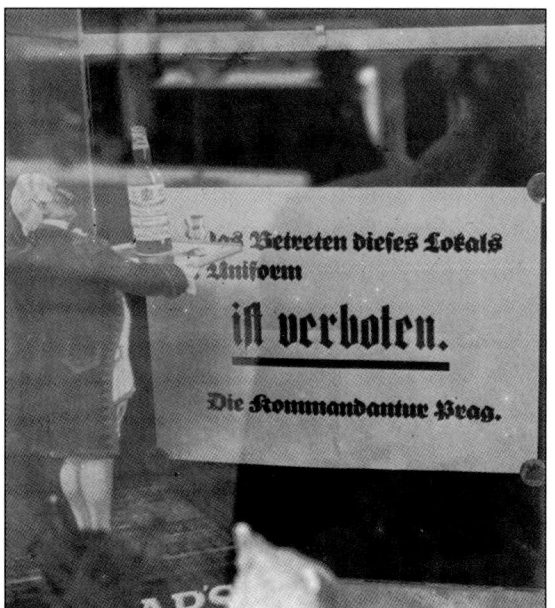

An official notice in a pub window announces that the establishment is out of bounds to troops in uniform

sending congratulations to the German Army on the fall of France. This was pure opportunism, for both Hácha and Eliáš were in contact with the Czech underground and with the exile movement under Beneš in Britain, now recognized as a provisional government. The tactic, however, was in tune with the public mood. As a Swedish correspondent reported in January 1941, the Czechs had 'found violent demonstrations ineffective' and were lying low to await 'a better opportunity'. Hitler was well-aware of the situation for the German Army had unearthed evidence of Eliáš' activities when it occupied Paris. But for the moment it suited him to curb the Gestapo terror. As he remarked in October 1940: 'The Government under Prime Minister Eliáš will continue to be

tolerated; accounts will be settled ... at a later stage.' As long as Czech wheels turned for German victory, opportunism served Nazi purposes just as well as honest collaboration. In the event of trouble, Hitler could always drop the moderate façade offered by Neurath and unleash the SS savagery represented by Frank.

The Czech underground recognized the reality of the situation and avoided dramatic action. Its activities were restricted to passive resistance, unattributable sabotage and intelligence gathering for the exile government in Britain. The Czechs participated in the 'V' campaign mounted by the BBC in January 1941 which called for the peoples of the occupied countries to paint the V for victory sign on walls and buildings under cover of the black-out. The slogan had a peculiar resonance for Czechs whose national motto was Pravda Vítězí (Truth Shall Prevail) and offered a form of resistance which was unlikely to provoke bloody reprisals. The campaign was so successful throughout occupied Europe that the Germans adopted it as their own. In the summer of 1941 Prague was suddenly decorated with huge V for Viktoria signs and banners proclaiming faith in German victory. It was an offence to deface, alter or ridicule a painted German 'V.' When this happened the entire neighbourhood was punished by a collective fine and confiscation of radio sets. Although they were still able to embarrass the Nazis in small ways, however, the screw was slowly tightening on the Czechs. A neutral journalist left a sad portrait of Prague in the spring of 1941. The centre of the city was crowded with German officers and arrogant party officials who monopolized the best hotels, cafés and restaurants. Nearly 120,000 of these people had arrived since the beginning of the occupation. Many of the civilians were carpetbaggers and war profiteers, earning an easy living in the bureaucracy or the armaments inspection. The statue of Jan Hus in Old Town Square was obscured by a massive hoarding advertising the Nazi Winterhilfe (Winter Help) campaign. The swastika fluttered from every flagpole. The Czechs, strangers in their own streets, boycotted the parades and festivals mounted by the Nazis. During the 'War Week Festival' in March, Germans were brought to the capital by train from all over the Protectorate. Uniformed children from the Hitler Youth and the League of German Girls marched and counter-marched through the Old Town, collecting for the German Army. The festival culminated in a communal Sunday meal in which only one course was eaten, supposedly as a sacrifice for German victory. Army canteens were brought into Wenceslas and Old Town Squares where long rows of tables and benches were set out. Soup and bread were served without ration cards and military bands played light music. Despite these inducements, however, most Czechs stayed at home and left the Germans to eat alone.

A huge V in Old Town Square proclaims official faith in German victory

On the eve of the invasion of Russia, there were signs of a new tilt of power towards Frank and the security police. In January 1941, Frank began a campaign against the Czech Legion, former soldiers who had deserted from the Habsburg Army during the First World War to fight for independence. The Legion had been banned in August 1939, but according to Frank its members were still secretly plotting against the Nazi New Order in association with the enemy abroad. There could be 'no constructive cooperation with the Reich' as long as they were at work. In the next few months over 8000 Legion veterans were purged from the Czech bureaucracy. But Frank remained unable to strike at his real target, General Eliáš, himself a former member of the Czech Legion. In May 1941, National Solidarity was purged. It had long been an object of suspicion by the Gestapo and its first secretary, Colonel Drgač, had been arrested as early as September 1939. He too had been a member of the Czech Legion. Now key positions were given to members of the 'Society for Cooperation with the Germans', an overtly collaborationist organization under Jan Fousek. Installed as head of NS, Fousek pledged to 'purify' the organization and turn it against 'incorrigibles' who still dreamed of independence. According to the Nazi controlled press, NS was at last becoming a tool 'to educate the Czech people into the ideology of National Socialism.'

As Hitler's panzers raced into Russia in June 1941, the full force of German propaganda in the Protectorate was directed against Bolshevism, a subject that had been played down during the period of the Nazi-Soviet pact. When the exile government in London signed an alliance with Russia shortly after the invasion, Beneš was denounced as a Communist tool. Hácha was quick to support Hitler's new crusade in the East. On 23 June, the day after the Nazi attack, he spoke on the radio, praising Hitler's decision 'to settle accounts with Bolshevism' and calling on Czechs 'to work with redoubled energy at the task entrusted to us of contributing to the food and armament programme of the Greater German Reich'. There was more than opportunism behind this appeal. Hácha was deeply hostile to Communism and suspicious of the new relationship with Stalin

The ubiquitous V sign appeared in every conceivable location, including public transport, all over the city

pursued by Beneš in London. The reaction of the population, however, was quite different. A powerful new enemy had entered the war against Germany, raising fresh hopes of liberation and revenge. Moreover Bohemia/Moravia was one of the few areas in East/Central Europe where Russia was genuinely popular. There had always been a strain of pan-Slavism in Czech politics and nobody had forgotten that apparently only the Soviet Union had been prepared to stand by Czechoslovakia during the Munich crisis of 1938. The Czech Communists capitalized on this mood, dropping their equivocal attitude to the occupation and moving into active opposition. The new mood was reflected in an outbreak of random sabotage throughout the Protectorate in which brake hoses were slashed on goods trains and military telephone lines were cut. In the factories many workers reported sick or slowed down production. In Prague there were brief strikes at the Vltava docks, the Avia aircraft factory and the Bohemia/Moravia engine works. Mass public demonstrations like those of autumn 1939, however, were avoided. The Czechs had learned the dangers of taking to the streets.

The Nazi invasion of the Soviet Union not only changed the atmosphere in Prague but also in London where the exile government was under increasing pressure to sabotage arms factories and railways in the Protectorate. Beneš felt that he had to respond lest Stalin shift his political support from the exile government to the Czech Communist leaders in Moscow. He was prepared to mount a sabotage campaign in the Protectorate, spearheaded by parachutists from Britain who would work with the home resistance. The Russians agreed to send similar teams to work with the communist underground. In August 1941 talks about cooperation took place between ÚVOD and the CPC.

A Prague shop window displays a collection of warm clothing for German troops in Russia

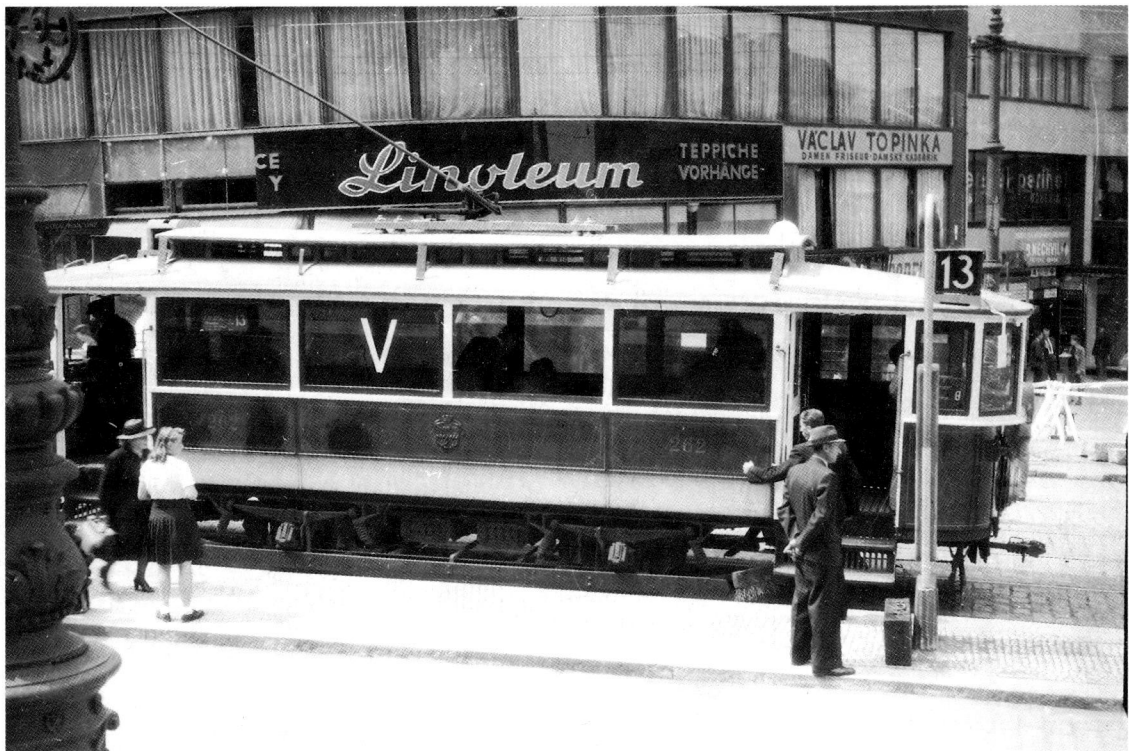

A wartime tram at the top of Wenceslas Square

Hybernská Street ▶ festooned with swastika flags

Meanwhile Beneš looked for some form of passive resistance which would demonstrate Czech solidarity with the allies and embarrass the Nazis without provoking reprisals on the scale of November 1939. As he remarked to a British official, Frank must not be given the excuse for another 'brutal and exemplary intervention'. On 14 September 1941 the Czech service of the BBC called for a boycott of the Protectorate press which had long since become a tool of the Nazis. According to Beneš this action was meant to serve two purposes. The first was as a test mobilization for an eventual uprising. The second was to show the Russians that the home population would obey the Czech service of the BBC, rather than the voice of Moscow Radio.

On 18 September, in the middle of this press boycott, the Prime Minister, General Eliáš, met three journalists led by Karel Lažnovský of *České Slovo,* one of the most notorious collaborators in Prague. Lažnovský had furthered his career by preaching solidarity with the Reich and praising the Nazi New Order on every possible occasion, rejecting the 'national idea' promoted by Palacký, Masaryk and Beneš. It was a bitter joke that his newspaper had even turned the Czech patron saint, Wenceslas, into a collaborator by claiming that he had stood for reconciliation with the Germans. Shortly after the meeting with Eliáš, Lažnovský collapsed and died. His two companions were also taken ill but survived. Although the Germans suspected that the three collaborators had been poisoned, nothing was ever proved. The incident, however, was added to the growing Gestapo file on Eliáš. Lažnovský was treated as a martyr, a symbol of Czech unity with the Reich. His wife was given a fat pension by the Nazis and a section of the Vltava embankment near the Palacký statue was renamed in his honour. It was a calculated insult to the memory of the man who had led the Czech national revival in the nineteenth century. Meanwhile the press boycott was brought to an end. By all accounts it had been a successful demonstration of passive resistance. Newspaper sales declined by over fifty per cent as the population displayed its silent contempt for the Nazis and their Czech collaborators. But it was to be the last significant act of mass resistance. With the German Army locked in the decisive struggle on the Eastern front, Hitler was not prepared to tolerate insubordination from the Czechs. The events of the summer had given Frank his golden opportunity – The day of the SS was about to dawn.

'The Führer told me before my departure [for Prague] :
"Wherever I see the unity of the Reich endangered,
I choose an SS leader and send him there to uphold the
unity of the Reich." From the Führer's words you can infer
the overall task of the SS and therefore what makes my own
task here a special one'

SS OBERGRUPPENFÜHRER REINHARD HEYDRICH :
SECRET SPEECH : 2 OCTOBER 1941

CHAPTER THREE

SS City

New recruits of the SS 'Totenkopf' Infantry Regiment take the oath of allegiance to Hitler in Old Town Square

IN MARCH 1939 Karl Hermann Frank became not only state secretary of the Protectorate but also Höhere SS und Polizei Führer (Higher SS and Police Leader – HSSPF). In his SS capacity Frank controlled the Nazi police system in Bohemia/Moravia and was answerable not to the Reichsprotektor, Neurath, but to Himmler and Heydrich in Berlin. Frank was used by his SS masters as a Trojan horse within the German bureaucracy. They had their own plans for the Protectorate which did not include Neurath and his old-fashioned civil servants. Himmler and Heydrich intended to transform Bohemia/Moravia into an SS state, breaking Czech resistance by a policy of selective terror. Frank was the ideal pawn in this political game. Installed at the Czernin Palace behind the Hradčany, he revelled in the trappings of power, the SS guards, the deferential servants, the opulent surroundings and the gleaming black Mercedes with the fluttering swastikas which sped him home each evening to his villa in Bubeneč with its collection of Nazi art. He was particularly proud of the communications room next to his office with direct telephone and teleprinter links to Berlin and all the capitals of occupied Europe. His salary increased in line with his responsibilities, rising with allowances to 50,000 Czech crowns. In 1940 Frank left his first wife for a younger woman who was considered something of a beauty and he enjoyed parading

An oil painting of an SS soldier which was displayed in the Prague headquarters of the Waffen SS

An elaborate SS ceremony in Old Town Square

her at formal events. He had come a long way from his beginnings as a humble bookseller in the Sudetenland. But he wanted more. Frank craved the post of Reichsprotektor and would do almost anything to achieve it. His driving ambition was used by Himmler and Heydrich, past masters at manipulating the weaknesses of others, to further their own sinister plans for Bohemia/Moravia.

Frank proved useful in promoting SS economic penetration of the Protectorate which was regarded as a key to the ultimate commercial domination of south-eastern Europe. Himmler's industrial empire was able to pick up expropriated Jewish property and other businesses owned by 'enemies of the state' under the guise of 'aryanization'. The SS was well represented in the furniture, ceramics and pharmaceutical industries, all of which were soon making large profits from German war orders. It also penetrated vital areas of the financial structure. Two of the largest finance houses in Prague, the Bohemia Discount Bank and the Bohemia Union Bank, were taken over by German banks linked to Himmler through the 'Friends of the Reichsführer SS', a group of businesses organized in 1934 to provide him with an SS slush fund. Through their shareholdings, these banks established a controlling interest in major Czech industries. The SS took over the Land Office in Prague established by the Czech government to administer state land reform. This was converted into an SS agency for settling Germans in the Protectorate following Hitler's decree of October 1939 appointing Himmler 'Reichs Commissioner for the Strengthening of German Nationhood'. In the long-term Bohemia/Moravia was to be broken up by bands of German settlement which would dominate and destroy the language and culture of the original inhabitants. Prague itself would become a completely German city. These SS economic activities offered irresistible opportunities for graft and corruption. In November 1939, it was officially announced that the head of the Land Office, SS Oberführer (Major General) Curt von Gottberg, had retired on the grounds of 'ill health'. In reality he had been unable to account for over one million Reichsmarks which had mysteriously vanished from his official accounts.

Frank played a key role in these SS plans. In August 1940 he produced a memorandum for Hitler on the fate of the Czech nation. This called for the ultimate Germanization of racially suitable Czechs and the extermination of the remainder. Meanwhile everything would be done to destroy the Czech 'national idea' and encourage collaboration with the Reich. The programme would be centrally administered from Prague, cloaked by the supposed commitment to Czech autonomy. In pursuing this line, Frank opposed demands from Nazi Party officials for the abolition of the Protectorate and its partition amongst the neighbouring German regions, a course that would have boosted the power of the Party bureaucracy at the expense of the SS. His former boss, Konrad Henlein, Gauleiter of the Sudetenland, was particularly anxious to establish his headquarters in Prague and lord it over the Czechs. Hitler approved of Frank's plans, confirming a longterm policy of destroying the Czech nation by assimilation, deportation, colonization and extermination. Although full implementation of this programme was to be delayed until after the war, it was a major

A day in the life of the Waffen SS - a page from the Nazi propaganda magazine Böhmen und Mähren *describing the routine at Ruzyně barracks*

victory for Frank and his SS masters in Berlin who were pulling the strings.

Himmler's military forces, the Waffen SS, entered Prague with the German Army on 15 March 1939. The Waffen SS established itself in the former Czech Army Staff College in Prague-Dejvice which was renamed the Adolf Hitler Barracks. The Charles University Law School on Nürnberger Street, near the Mendel Bridge, became an SS headquarters. The building was requisitioned after the student troubles of November 1939, turning this section of the city into an SS enclave. In April 1939 two battalions of the SS

The 'Totenkopf' band outside the SS headquarters housed in the former Law Faculty of Charles University

Waffen SS

Verteilung von SS-Schrifttum an die Männer, darunter „Sieg der Waffen, Sieg des Kindes".
Unten: Beim Mittagessen / Bekleidungsappell / Übung der Meldefahrer / Scharfschießen / Antreten nach dem Gefechtsexerzieren / Beim Dienst der Musiker

K. H. Frank takes the salute at Hitler's birthday parade near Old Town Square

'Germania' Regiment were posted to Prague as guards for the Reichsprotektor. Two months later they were replaced by troops of the Leibstandarte Adolf Hitler. Thereafter Waffen SS units were regularly rotated through Prague. The presence of their men in the striped sentry boxes outside the Hradčany Castle and the regular Saturday parade of the guard battalion down Wenceslas Square were permanent reminders to Czechs and Germans alike of the reality of SS power. In the following years the Waffen SS presence continued to expand. In 1942, 37,000 Czechs were expelled from their villages when a vast SS military exercise area was established near Benešov, south-west of Prague. By 1944 15,000 SS troops were training there and another 7000 were posted in or around Prague. The rear area medical services also moved in, taking over the large hospital near the Vltava at Vyšehrad in the summer of 1941 for SS casualties from the bitter battles on the Eastern Front. Himmler was interested not only in the economic resources of Bohemia/Moravia but also in its reserves of German manpower, raising two SS regiments in the Protectorate. In September 1944, these men were brought together as the 31st SS Volunteer Grenadier Division Böhmen-Mähren which was destroyed in the last-ditch battles for Hungary and Moravia.

The SS exploited the spectacular backdrop provided by Prague for parades and ceremonies. In May 1942 SS volunteers marched

up Nürnbergerstrasse to the Old Town Square where they took their oath of allegiance to Hitler and heard a speech by Frank on Bolshevism and the world Jewish conspiracy. The occasion was covered by a special issue of *Böhmen und Mähren* (Bohemia and Moravia), a lavishly produced monthly magazine published by Frank in his capacity as State Secretary. The journal, which regularly promoted the claims of the SS to a leading role in the Nazi New Order, saluted the heroism of the Waffen SS on the Eastern Front. Besides an extensive photo spread of the ceremony in Old Town Square, *Böhmen und Mähren* provided an account of a typical day in the life of an SS soldier, from reveille and morning parade, through firing practice and gymnastics to evening roll-call and lights out. The pictures suggested that the off-duty SS man liked to relax with a copy of *Böhmen und Mähren*. The reality was different. A secret document photographed by an employee of the Prague Electricity Company recorded what happened in November 1939 when nine members of the élite Leibstandarte Adolf Hitler spent the evening in a pub near the barracks at Prague-Ruzyně. After consuming large quantities of Czech beer, they staggered into the road and began shooting out streetlights with their revolvers, destroying twelve and leaving the pavement littered with spent cartridge cases. Running out of ammunition, they proceeded to tear down seventy metres of wire netting around some allotments before uprooting a heavy wooden fence. Arriving at a level-crossing just as a train was passing, they rounded off the evening by bouncing on the barrier pole, breaking it in several places. The damage caused by their drunken escapade ran into thousands of Czech crowns. The whole embarrassing affair, so damaging to the official SS image, had to be quickly hushed up.

Frank made no secret of his contempt for his nominal boss Neurath and the bureaucrats in the Reichsprotektor's office. He regarded

K. H. Frank makes a speech to SS recruits in Old Town Square

them as soft and vacillating, unworthy representatives of the Nazi Order. As long as Neurath remained at the Hradčany, however, he was a barrier to the goal of total SS power. With the encouragement of Himmler and Heydrich in Berlin, Frank plotted constantly against the Reichsprotektor, assuming that with Neurath out of the way he would be the natural SS candidate to run Bohemia/Moravia. This had been Frank's aim during the demonstrations in autumn 1939 when his police had deliberately provoked a riot. But there were no more mass demonstrations and Hitler was unwilling to launch a final crushing blow against the Czechs. The wave of petty sabotage and the press boycott of September 1941, however, offered new possibilities for intrigue. With the assistance of his security chiefs, Frank compiled a dossier which argued that the Protectorate was on the verge of rebellion. Unless total power was granted to the SS, the Czechs would stab the German Army in the back at a crucial stage of the war. Frank's report was based on suspect and often manufactured evidence. The most dramatic incidents in the summer of 1941, the destruction of a large petrol dump and a dynamite attack on a German children's home, were probably the work, not of the Czech resistance, but of the Gestapo.

On 21 September 1941, Frank brought this dossier to Hitler's field headquarters, the Wolf's Lair, in East Prussia, where his boss, Heydrich, briefed the Führer about the situation. Hitler flew into a rage, complaining that the Czechs had confused leniency with weakness. They regarded Neurath as an amiable old gentleman and took his goodwill for stupidity. They had to be taught a lesson. Two days later Hitler ordered Neurath to

A series of pictures covering the inauguration of the acting Reichsprotector Reinhard Heydrich at Prague Castle on 28 September 1941

take a vacation. His policies had failed and someone else must do the job. Frank believed that the great prize was now within his grasp. But he was disappointed. Although Hitler was prepared to hand over the Protectorate to the SS, he did not intend to name a mere Sudeten as his representative. Instead he appointed Heydrich as acting Reichsprotektor. Hitler's choice vested authority in the architect of the Gestapo terror, a man widely regarded as the most dangerous in occupied Europe. Heydrich had plotted to replace Neurath from the beginning, using Frank as his tool. He dreamed of transforming Bohemia/Moravia into a model SS state, the springboard to total power in the Nazi New Order. Frank had been duped by someone for whom conspiracy was second nature. The Czechs learned their fate on Saturday 27 September 1941 when the controlled press carried a stunning and unexpected announcement: 'The Reichsprotektor of Bohemia/Moravia, Herr Konstantin von Neurath, has had to suggest to the Führer that he be given leave on medical grounds... Under the circumstances the Führer could not refuse... and has entrusted SS Obergruppenführer and General of Police Reinhard Heydrich with the performance of the duties of the Reichsprotektor for Bohemia/Moravia.' The news confirmed the triumph of the SS in the long struggle to dominate the Protectorate and spelled the doom of the home resistance.

As the official announcement was published, Heydrich arrived in Prague by plane, landing at Ruzyně, and spending the night at the Esplanade Hotel. The following morning he was officially welcomed by Frank at the Hradčany Castle. The timing was probably deliberate for 28 September was the feast day

of St Wenceslas, the patron saint of the Czechs. The black flag of the SS with its sinister silver runes was hoisted over Prague and the new acting Reichsprotektor reviewed a Waffen SS guard of honour while a band played the 'Horst Wessel Song,' the official Nazi anthem. A curfew was imposed and martial law proclaimed. Special courts were established which imposed summary justice on those accused of threatening the political or economic security of the Protectorate. The tomb of the unknown soldier in Old Town Square, a focus of Czech national sentiment since the beginning of the occupation, was demolished. The resistance, which had been thoroughly penetrated by Gestapo spies, was smashed within weeks of Heydrich's arrival. The first parachute group from the Soviet Union was swept up in the police dragnet as was the first Czech parachutist from Britain who was arrested on 25 October when he visited an address under surveillance by the Gestapo. By the end of November nearly 5000 suspects had been arrested and over 400 death sentences passed. The real total was much higher for many more were murdered in police custody or at Mauthausen concentration camp. The police terror was designed not only to crush the resistance but also to pave the way for ultimate Germanization. Former army officers and intellectuals, regarded by the Nazis as the natural leaders of the Czech nation, were amongst the main victims.

In a secret speech to Nazi officials on 2 October, Heydrich left his audience in no doubt that the SS was now in control and set out two goals for the future. The short-term aim was to mobilize Czech workers and industry behind the Nazi blitzkrieg in Russia. The long-term aim was the ultimate German-

The Reichsfürer SS Heindrich Himmler arriving at Prague Castle on 29 October 1941

ization of the Czech 'rabble'. Racially suitable candidates would be absorbed. The remainder would be deported to the East, a euphemism for extermination. No hint of this second goal must be allowed to leak out. Until the end of the war the Czechs would be encouraged to identify survival with subservience. In the next few months, Heydrich set out to depoliticize the Czechs. He did not believe that they would ever love him but that was irrelevant. What was important was that they should work for Germany. This involved the use of both the carrot and the stick. If resistance was punished, collaboration was rewarded. Heydrich increased rations for workers in heavy industry and arranged for the distribution of confiscated black-market food to the canteens of the arms factories. Workers were also given bigger allowances of tobacco and shoes. Press and radio propaganda condemned the 'fools' in the resistance who would bring nothing but grief to themselves and their nation and urged the Czechs to follow the example of St Wenceslas who had supposedly committed the future of his people to the German Reich.

Heydrich's arrival terrified the German bureaucrats at the office of the Reichsprotektor who did not know what might happen to them. He had brought his own SS staff from Berlin and rarely consulted the career civil servants whom he despised. One of them, a cousin of the writer Thomas Mann, panicked and fled to Switzerland. The Czech government was totally demoralized. The Prime Minister, General Alois Eliáš, was arrested in front of his office and sentenced to death by a Special Session of the Nazi People's Court for his secret links with the Czech government in exile. He was then

Heydrich at a gala evening concert in the Rudolfinum

held as a hostage for the good behaviour of his colleagues. The State President, Emil Hácha, called on the Czechs to abandon any thought of resistance and collaborate for the sake of national survival. Under the new SS regime, Czech autonomy rapidly became a fiction. According to Heydrich the Protectorate regime must no longer be an agency for conveying Czech complaints to the Germans, but a transmission belt conveying German orders to the Czechs. On 19 November 1941, in the baroque splendour of St Vitus Cathedral, high above Prague, Hácha gave Heydrich the seven keys to the jewel room containing the crown of St Wenceslas, the most precious possession of the Czech nation, as a symbol of subservience to Nazi Germany. In January 1942 the government was reorganized. Dr Jaroslav Krejčí became Prime Minister but he was almost powerless. A German, Walter Bertsch, was installed as Minister of Economy and Labour and all cabinet meetings were henceforth conducted in German. Significantly Bertsch was given the honourary rank of SS Oberführer (Major General). Under Bertsch, Czech companies were amalgamated or closed to suit German needs and Czech labour was conscripted for war work both in the Protectorate and in Germany.

The leading Czech quisling, Emmanuel Moravec, was appointed Minister of Education and Popular Enlightenment, feeding the population a regular diet of pro-Nazi propaganda. Under Moravec, Czech children were to be taught only what was necessary to equip them for a future as workers in the Nazi New Order. Through compulsory membership of collaborationist youth organizations and later labour service in Germany, it was planned to free Czech children from the influence of parents and teachers, transforming them into a new generation committed to the victory of the Reich. As Heydrich emphasized on 4 February 1942, it was 'essential first to pounce upon the Czech teachers who constitute ... a training corps for opposition. We must clearly smash it ... and abolish Czech higher schools. The Czech youth will then undoubtedly have to be rallied somewhere in a way so as to make it possible to educate it outside of school and remove it from out of this atmosphere ... this can doubtless be best done in the field of sports. In physical training and sport we shall therefore ... make possible a transformation, a re-education, an education altogether.' As for the Czech universities, those breeding grounds of resistance and dissent, they must never rise again. A suitable excuse would be found to keep them closed once the three-year ban of November 1939 expired. Moravec would see to it. These plans for Czech youth combined undermining resistance, providing labour and paving the way for post-war Germanization, Heydrich's three main tasks in Bohemia/Moravia.

Heydrich boasted that he had totally integrated the Protectorate into the German war effort. Resistance was crushed and order reigned. His work was admired by the Nazi leadership. On 23 January 1942, Hitler registered his approval of SS rule : 'Neurath let himself be completely diddled ... Another six months of that regime and production would have fallen by 25 per cent. Of all the Slavs, the Czech is most dangerous, because he's a worker. He has a sense of discipline, he's orderly ... he knows how to hide his plans. Now they'll work for they know we're pitless and cruel.' According to the Propaganda Minister, Goebbels, Heydrich's policy was 'a truly model one ... As a result the Protectorate is now in the best of spirits, quite in contrast to other occupied or annexed areas.' SS influence continued to expand. The signs were evident everywhere in Prague, from the black flags at the Hradčany to the new dominance of the security police in Protectorate politics. Now more than ever

The Czech Minister Emmanuel Moravec at an athletics display

the Petschek Palace was a place of terror for ordinary Czechs. In March 1942, Heydrich opened a new Reich Security School in Prague, delivering his inaugural address beneath a bust of Hitler. The cadets were to pursue their grisly police career throughout the occupied East. SS economic influence continued to grow. In December 1941 Heydrich hosted a conference in the Spanish Hall of the Hradčany Castle on the role of the Protectorate in the economies of southeastern Europe. In this period too he was plotting along with Himmler to divert Czech arms production, which amounted to one-third of the total arms production of occupied Europe, to serve the needs of the Waffen SS. This bitter battle for control of the Czech weapons industry, which pitted the SS against both the Army and the new Armaments Ministry under Albert Speer, continued until the closing months of the war.

Heydrich had grandiose plans for Prague which he intended to transform into one of the leading cities of the Nazi New Order, the gateway to an SS empire in the Balkans and the occupied East. It was to become one of the great cities of the Reich, as German as Berlin, Munich or Cologne. A radical approach to the Czech population had to await the end of the war, but in the meantime Heydrich attempted to transform the city into a centre of German art and culture. He patronized the German University which was expanded to serve the needs of the SS racial mission in the East, founding new chairs for a series of SS approved academics. He also promoted Prague as a centre of German music, 'Mozart's second home', and built up the German Philharmonic Orchestra. In May 1941, German became the sole language of the Prague city government. Heydrich dreamed of turning the city into a monument to his own greatness with the assistance of Hitler's personal architect, and later Minister of Armaments, Albert Speer. In consultation with Speer, he planned to rebuild Prague, like Berlin, in the Nazi imperial style, with a modern German opera house and a new government complex around the Hradčany Castle. The city was to be encircled by a massive ring road and linked to Berlin and other major cities by a series of a new autobahns. Fortunately shortages of labour and construction materials meant that little could be done to implement these megalomaniacal schemes and Prague was spared the vulgarity and crude gigantism typical of Nazi architecture.

The assassination of Heydrich by two parachute agents sent by the Czech government in exile in London did nothing to shake the reality of SS power. Heydrich was wounded on the morning of 27 May 1942 by a bomb attack on his car as it rounded a tight corner

A reconstruction of the bomb attack on Heydrich on 27 May 1942

into V Holešovičkách in the suburb of Prague-Libeň. He was rushed to the nearby Bulovka Hospital where he died in the early hours of 4 June from infected wounds. Heydrich was the only leading Nazi to be assassinated during the Second World War. Prague became the backdrop for ostentatiously staged SS mourning rites. On the evening of 5 June, the body was moved from the Bulovka Hospital to the Hradčany through streets lined with SS men bearing flaming torches. By precise timing the coffin passed through the castle gates as midnight chimed from the spires and towers of the city below, ghostly and still under German curfew. Heydrich lay in state in the first courtyard for two days under the black banners of the SS, guarded by senior officers of the security police, while endless rows of Czechs filed past, paying homage to their oppressor. It was a carefully organized propaganda scene which was captured by a special issue of *Böhmen und Mähren*. On 7 June, after a ceremony at the Hradčany attended by Himmler, the coffin was paraded on a gun carriage across the Charles Bridge and through the Old Town to the main station where a special funeral train was waiting to take Heydrich on his last journey to Berlin.

Meanwhile terror stalked the streets of Prague as the SS took savage reprisals for the death of their hero. In the morning and in the evening the firing squads were busy at the German execution grounds in Prague-Kobylisy. A huge reward was posted for information leading to the capture of the assassins and the evidence found at the scene of the attack was displayed in the windows of the Baťa shoe store at the bottom of Wenceslas Square. Anyone with information about these items was to report to the police. Those concealing knowledge of the assassins were to be shot along with their entire families. On the evening of 9 June, shortly after Heydrich's funeral, Hitler decided to teach the Czechs a final lesson in submission and humility. At the suggestion of Horst Böhme, the commander of the Nazi security police in the Protectorate, he ordered the total destruction of Lidice, a village near Prague, which was wrongly suspected by the Gestapo of having some connection with Heydrich's assassins. One hundred and seventy-three men were shot on the spot by the SS. Another eleven who were not in the village that evening were arrested and murdered soon afterwards as were eight men and seven women already under arrest because they had relations serving with the army in exile in Britain. Two hundred and three women were deported to concentration camps. One hundred and five children were separated from their parents. A few, considered racially

A Gestapo photograph of the bomb damage to Heydrich's car

A Czech newspaper announces the attack on Heydrich and the proclamation of Martial Law

German wounded pass Heydrich's coffin with its SS guard of honour

Heydrich's coffin passing over Charles Bridge on its final journey to Berlin

Heydrich's body lying in state at Hradčany Castle while thousands of Czechs terrified of German reprisals file past

In their frantic search for Heydrich's assassins, the Gestapo circulated photographs of the objects left at the scene of the attack

suitable for Germanization, were handed over to SS families. The remainder were swallowed up by the concentration-camp system. Only one hundred and fifty-three women and seventeen children returned after the war. The empty buildings were destroyed and the village levelled to the ground. Frank boasted that corn would grow where Lidice once stood as a reminder of the fate awaiting those who defied Nazi rule. In the aftermath of Lidice, rumours were deliberately planted that every tenth Czech would be shot unless the assassins surrendered. On 15 June, infuriated by the continuing failure of the Gestapo to find the parachutists, Himmler called for an intensification of the SS terror, ordering Frank to arrest and murder 30,000 politically active Czechs. This final step proved unnecessary. On 18 June, betrayed by one of their comrades, Heydrich's assassins, along with five other Czech parachutists, were cornered in the Cathedral Church of St Cyril and St Methodius on Ressel Street. After a gun battle with an assault force of Waffen SS from the Prague guard battalion, they committed suicide rather than surrender.

The mood of national relief was obvious. Two weeks after the battle on Ressel Street, on 3 July 1942, over 200,000 Czechs packed Wenceslas Square and sang the national

The bodies of the men of Lidice murdered as a reprisal for the killing of Heydrich

anthem whilst giving the Hitler salute and pledging allegiance to the Third Reich. It was the lowest point of the occupation. The assassination and its aftermath had shattered organized resistance and cowed the population. Many sought protection by taking German classes or subscribing to German newspapers but everyone was at risk from an SS murder campaign which struck at random. Frank had always argued for a policy of selective terror and boasted of its success but he remained a frustrated man. When Heydrich was attacked, Frank believed that his hour had come. He confidently expected to be appointed as the new Acting Reichsprotektor. Once again, however, he was robbed of the great prize. Hitler nominated another SS general, Obergruppenführer Kurt Daluege of the uniformed police, in Heydrich's place. Frank resented Daluege and pressed Himmler to remove him, arguing that he did not understand the Czechs. The Reichsführer SS refused and Daluege remained in office despite the ravages of a progressive brain disorder, probably caused by syphilis. He was finally replaced in August 1943 when Hitler appointed Wilhelm Frick as the last Reichsprotektor. Frick had just been ousted by Himmler as Minister of the Interior and was shunted off to Prague as a consolation prize. The post was purely ceremonial for Hitler issued a decree concentrating all real power in the German State Secretary. Frick had the right to pardon persons convicted of

The bodies of Heydrich's assassins are identified for the Gestapo

The Orthodox Cathedral of St Cyril and St Methodius on Ressel Street which provided a refuge for Heydrich's assassins

A Czech magazine cover showing the demonstration of loyalty to the Reich in Wenceslas Square in July 1942; this was the lowest point of the occupation

crimes against the state but this was 'a privilege which he never seems to have exercised'. Frank had at last achieved political supremacy and the rank of SS Obergruppenführer (General) but the title he really coveted had finally eluded him.

In the closing years of German rule, Heydrich was treated as a Nazi martyr, a symbol of the indissoluable union between Bohemia/Moravia and the Reich. On 18 October 1942 a section of the Vltava embankment was named after him in the presence of his widow. It was probably no accident that one part of the new 'Reinhard Heydrich Ufer' had previously been named after František Palacký and the other, near the National Theatre, after Tomáš Masaryk. The whole affair was a carefully calculated symbol of Nazi supremacy. According to Frank everyone who used the street could look up at the castle, the seat of German power, and remember Heydrich's work for Bohemia/Moravia. At a second ceremony a monument bearing Heydrich's death mask was unveiled at the fatal corner on V Holešovičkách with a perpetual SS guard of honour. Passers-by had to remove their hats as a sign of respect for the dead hero. At the same time the SS founded The Reinhard Heydrich Foundation in Prague dedicated to the study of 'ethnic, economic and cultural problems' in the territories 'for which he fought and fell'. The activities of these SS 'experts' remain obscure although one of their tasks was to produce pamphlets for Waffen SS troops on the Eastern Front covering subjects like 'ethnic biology and ethnic-leadership'. At a special conference held by the Foundation in Prague in February 1944, the SS laid claim to the direction of all German academic work concerning the occupied Eastern territories. Meanwhile Frank continued to pursue the goal of long-term Germanization as head of a special staff 'for the strengthening of the German Race' established at the Hradčany Castle. According to Frank, SS power provided an absolute guarantee against trouble from the Czechs. The secret police had the resistance under control and any rising would be immediately crushed by the Waffen SS.

As Frank emphasized, Heydrich's appointment was a turning point in the affairs of Bohemia/Moravia. After 1941 the Protectorate regime was nothing but a Nazi puppet. Hácha, old and sick, was often confined to a wheelchair. He still believed that he was shielding his people from the Nazi terror but opportunism had long since become subservience. As late as 20 April 1945, he sent an obsequious telegram to Hitler in the ruins of Berlin, congratulating the Führer on his birthday. Hácha's ministers became mere mouthpieces for the Germans, used to

An idealized commemoration portrait of Heydrich

Kurt Daluege, head of the Ordnungspolizei - the Nazi uniformed police and Heydrich's successor as acting Reichsprotektor

denounce the exiles abroad and urge the people to work for German victory. In December 1943, they participated in a propaganda campaign against the Czech-Soviet Pact just concluded by Beneš in Moscow. The exiles were condemned as tools of the international Communist conspiracy who had betrayed their country to Stalin. On 19 December 1943, a new organization, The League Against Bolshevism, was founded to preach this message. It was designed to counter Communist propaganda, divide the Czech people, and drive a wedge between the population at home and the exiles in London and Moscow. The Germans hoped that middle-class Czechs would join and released a number of conservatives from concentration camps as a conciliatory gesture. The organization spread stories of Soviet atrocities, mounted anti-Communist exhibitions, published pamphlets and arranged book displays. Posters and lectures portrayed the German Army in the East as the last barrier against barbarism, fighting heroically for European civilization. Anti-Semitism was deployed against the emerging Czech-Soviet alliance, utilizing the fact that many of the soldiers in the Czech Army on the Eastern front, under General Ludvík Svoboda, were Jewish. In March 1943, after the battle of Sokolovo, the first major action fought by Svoboda's men, Frank published the accounts of six captured soldiers who denounced the force as 'a Jewish-Czech unit', part of the world Jewish conspiracy against the Nazi New Order.

An advertisement for the Škoda Company, the biggest arms producer in the Protectorate

When the allied bombing campaign intensified after 1942, important German factories were evacuated to the Protectorate. As part of this process a branch of the Junkers aircraft works was established in Prague. The mobilization of Czech workers initiated by Heydrich continued. Some were sent to Germany but the majority were assigned to factories in Bohemia/Moravia. In 1944 there was a new wave of closures as inessential businesses were shut down to release labour for war work. At the same time the struggle between the SS and the Armaments Ministry under Speer for control of Czech weapons production was fought to a bitter conclusion. As part of this competition, Speer unsuccessfully attempted to poach SS Oberführer Bertsch, Minister of Industry and Labour in the Protectorate regime. By the end of 1944 the SS had finally emerged triumphant, but it was an empty victory as allied armies closed in from East and West on the ruins of the Reich. After the war, Speer complained that his experiences at the hands of Himmler and Frank in the battle over armaments had resembled the worst nightmares of Franz Kafka.

Heydrich's youth policy also continued after his death. The universities remained closed and the secondary schools were flooded with new books emphasizing loyalty to the Reich and denouncing the Czech 'national idea'. A youth movement was established under a former Czech athlete, Dr František Teuner, dedicated to the cult of physical fitness and the propagation of Nazi ideas. An annual sports week was initiated in Prague for children from all over the Protectorate. The first of these, in December 1942, was attended by 60,000 boys and girls. The last, held in June 1944, began with a parade through Wenceslas Square and speeches by Frank, Moravec and Teuner. Sporting

A Heydrich commemoration stamp based on the death mask made for Himmler

The winners of a swimming competition at the Barrandov open-air swimming pool during the annual Youth Sports Festival

competitions were held throughout the city. These included canoeing on the Vltava and swimming at the pool beneath the Terraces in the smart suburb of Prague-Barrandov. The uniforms, flags, badges and set-piece gymnastic displays were closely modelled on those of the Hitler Youth as was the cult of the athletic body. The Reich was elevated as a metaphor of the modern. Czech culture was reduced to the wearing of quaint folk costumes, a step foreseen by Heydrich as an important move towards Germanization. Despite its emphasis on what the Nazis called the 'Reich idea', the security police kept a close watch on the youth movement, fearing that it might be turned to nationalist purposes. The whole educational programme,

like everything else in the Protectorate, began to run down towards the end of the war. By the beginning of 1945 the secondary schools were closed and the 'Reich idea' was nearing the end of its active life.

Far from the fronts and threatened by a renewal of the Gestapo terror, few Czechs were prepared to take risks until the day of liberation dawned. As one report remarked, people believed in allied victory but were 'afraid of what the Germans may do to them in the meantime'. The Nazis dealt harshly with any sign of opposition. On 24 August 1943, 400 workers at the Bohemia/Moravia Engine Factory went on strike. The Prague Gestapo responded by shooting the four ringleaders and sentencing fourteen others to long terms of hard labour. It was all over within three hours. In 1944 Frank had gallows erected in the arms factories as a deterrent against sabotage and industrial action. Informers were everywhere and underground groups went in constant danger of betrayal. A message from Prague in May 1943 warned Beneš that German terrorism made it extremely difficult to recruit underground workers. Although executions were no longer running at the same level as directly after the Heydrich assassination, the SS was still shooting 150 Czechs a week. In July 1943, a British Foreign Office report noted that the Nazis had killed or tortured 50,000 Czechs since the beginning of the occupation. The dead 'made up the most active and resolute patriots, the bitterest enemies of Germany', a fact that had 'reduced the strength of the most actively aggressive elements to a large extent'.

It was against this depressing background that resistance networks were painfully rebuilt in the last years of the occupation. In the non-Communist underground a new central organization, the PRNV (National Revolutionary Preparatory Committee), emerged to replace ÚVOD which had been decimated in 1942. In June 1944 the PRNV shared the fate of its predecessor when the Gestapo arrested almost 300 of its members. The ON continued to exist, building resistance cells in the police, Protectorate guard and fire brigade. In the middle of 1943, however, the Germans uncovered one of its networks and captured many hidden weapons. Rada Tří (The Council of Three), founded in the summer of 1944 by former members of ON and PVVZ, was penetrated within months. By December 1944, 320 of its members had been rounded up and imprisoned. The Communists had no better luck and their clandestine groups were repeatedly smashed. In August 1944 the Germans launched a new version of Operation Gitter (Operation Fence) which netted 44 leaders of the party in Prague. In this situation sabotage and other forms of overt action were never a serious threat to Nazi rule. Passive resistance was more common, particularly when it became clear after mid-1944 that Hitler was losing the war. Many fled to the countryside to avoid compulsory labour service or reported themselves as unfit for work. In October 1944 the Junkers factory in Prague-Vysočany was operating with only 82 per cent of its work force. At the end of the year the average sick rate throughout the armaments industry was 10 per cent.

Although Frank still held Bohemia/Moravia with an iron hand the SS dream was already fading. By autumn 1944 the Western allies had broken out of the Normandy beach-head and were approaching the German border. In the East the Red Army had cleared Hitler's armies from the Ukraine and had entered Poland and Hungary. German refugees fleeing allied bombing and the advancing Russians began to flood into the Protectorate. In September there were uprisings behind the Nazi lines in both Warsaw and Slovakia

A propaganda display in the windows of the League Against Bolshevism - a collaborationist organization founded by the Nazis

'The Soviet Paradise' - a propaganda exhibition staged in the winter of 1941

which the SS suppressed with savage fury. On 15 November Prague was bombed for the first time. The mood of the occupiers changed as defeat drew nearer. Conscious of the blood they had shed, they feared a terrible Czech revenge. As early as May 1944, Frank disarmed the small force of Czech government troops which served as Hácha's ceremonial guard. It was known that resistance cells were active in its ranks and Frank feared it might provide armed support for a Czech rebellion. Five thousand were sent to Italy as a labour battalion. A token force of 1,500 remained in Prague under tight supervision. In June 1944 Heydrich's widow withdrew her sons from the Hitler Youth because she felt that it was too dangerous for German boys to walk the streets of the city in the blackout. She also complained about threatening letters and Himmler ordered increased security at her estate in Panenské Břežany, twelve miles outside Prague, Hitler's 'perpetual gift' to the Heydrich family.

When the Slovak rising began, Frank wrote to Himmler demanding quick and brutal action before the Czechs were infected with the spirit of rebellion: 'The response is great among the Czech population. I am convinced that events will develop into a dangerous situation unless the revolt in Slovakia is quickly put down... One cannot lose one minute.' At the same time Frank moved against the police, the only organized

Czech force that remained in the Protectorate. Their rifles were confiscated and they were allowed only pistols with limited amounts of ammunition. The weapons had to be handed in at the end of each shift with every round accounted for. Special SS battle-groups were despatched to the Slovakian border to prevent guerrilla bands from entering Bohemia/Moravia. On 3 November 1944 Frank ordered that anyone caught in the area attempting to evade labour service or to join the partisans was to be publicly hanged : 'They bodies must be left on the gallows for 48 hours in public view . . . they will be guarded by Czech gendarmes to prevent their being cut down under any circumstances.'

Frank's forebodings were shared at the highest levels of the SS. In November 1944, alarmed by the Warsaw Uprising, Himmler ordered Frank to take the strictest precautions against a similar outbreak in Prague, another ancient city where sewers and unknown tunnels might harbour a secret army. SS officers who had fought against the Poles were transfered to Prague, including SS Obergruppenführer Paul Giebel of the uniformed police who had commanded a battle squad in Warsaw. From his headquarters in Prague-Dejvice, the Waffen SS commander, Gruppenführer (Lieutenant-General) Karl-Friedrich von Pückler, ordered the formation of improvised combat groups from SS training establishments and reserve troops around the city, ready to intervene in any emergency. Even in this final phase, with nemesis approaching from both East and West, Frank continued to struggle for total SS power, resisting attempts to create units of the Volkssturm, the German home guard, in the Protectorate. This force was headed by Nazi Party officials and was thus regarded as a threat to SS control. Instead German civilians in Prague were encouraged to form armed self-defence squads

The Waffen SS commander von Pückler visiting an officer training school in Prague. His staff car is a Czech Tatra which was popular with SS officers

The Head of the Russian National Liberation Committee General Andrei Vlasov (in glasses) with K. H. Frank at Hradčany Castle in November 1944

German military signs were in evidence all over the city. A black arrow on the lamp-post points to a Waffen SS establishment

and move into designated apartment blocks for mutual protection. In their free hours these so-called 'alarm groups' were expected to guard offices, factories and German residential areas. They were equipped from reserve stocks or weapons captured from the Slovak army.

As the foundations of Nazi Germany crumbled, Prague became the scene of a final bizarre ceremony orchestrated by the SS. Himmler, like Hitler, had always argued that the task of the New Order in the East was to make the Russians slaves of the master race. For this reason he had opposed attempts to create a Russian national liberation movement, dedicated to the destruction of Communism, a course favoured by many German army officers. Volunteers attached to German units were not formed into Russian divisions. Regarded by Hitler as inherently untrustworthy, they were transferred to the Western Front in 1943. The leader of the Russian national liberation movement, Andrei Vlasov, a former Soviet general captured near Leningrad in July 1942, was denounced by Himmler as a swine and a traitor. This line was echoed by Frank who feared that any endorsement of self-determination in the East would give the Czechs dangerous ideas. In his own sphere he had bitterly opposed the military exploitation of Czech manpower, either in the flak defences or as volunteers on the Eastern front. According to Frank, the Czechs were untrustworthy and would defect at the first opportunity, an argument with which Hitler agreed. As the fortunes of war swung against the Nazis, however, Himmler had second thoughts about the Russians. On 16 September 1944 he met Vlasov for the first time and pledged his support for the formation of a Russian National Liberation Committee (KNOR) with its own armed forces.

On 14 November 1944, Vlasov's manifesto was proclaimed in Prague, the only Slav city still in German hands after the fall of Warsaw. Vlasov arrived by train from Berlin just before dawn and was driven to the nearby Alcron Hotel. Later that morning an official car took him up the hill to the Hradčany for breakfast with Frank. The Russian then inspected an SS guard of honour in the castle courtyard, following the example of Himmler and Heydrich in the heady days of unchallenged Nazi power. Shortly after midday, in the Spanish Hall, a favourite setting for SS ceremonies, Frank introduced Vlasov and his KNOR to a Russian audience, which had been assembled from anti-Communist refugees, slave labourers and prisoners of war. Vlasov was disappointed that neither Himmler nor any other leading figure in the German government had turned up for the occasion, and regarded Frank as decidedly second-rate. As for Frank, he clearly had reservations about his strange new ally and gave an unconvincing performance. The dangers of endorsing Russian liberation while continuing to repress the Czechs probably occupied his mind. But like his master Himmler, Frank was prepared to gamble on a final desperate throw of the dice. Already denounced as a war criminal for his role in the destruction of Lidice, he could feel the noose tightening around his own neck. That evening Frank hosted a banquet for the Russians at which the wine and brandy flowed freely. It was the last great state occasion of his murderous career. Within months Vlasov's army was to turn on its reluctant SS allies and play a key role in the final liberation of Prague from the terror that had gripped the city for six long years.

'The building requisitioned by the Gestapo for its headquarters in Prague was a huge gloomy structure in the street called Bredovská... Its high hall and corridors seemed dark even on a summer afternoon... In crossing the hall it was impossible not to think of the cellars underneath, where perhaps at that very moment human beings were being flogged to death for no other reason than that they were Czechs, Jews or Communists.'

SIR PAUL DUKES: *AN EPIC OF THE GESTAPO*

CHAPTER FOUR

The Palace of Death

The Petschek Palace - the grim headquarters of the Prague Gestapo

Reinhard Heydrich (the head of the Reich's Central Security Office which included the Gestapo) in consultation with K. H. Frank (the Higher SS and Police Leader in the Protectorate), planning their reign of terror

THE GERMAN occupation destroyed the rule of law and substituted a totalitarian legal system based on Nazi ideology. Under the Protectorate the life and liberty of the subject enjoyed few safeguards and whole groups of people, beginning with the Jews, were arbitrarily deprived of their rights. The process began almost immediately. The decree establishing the Protectorate of 16 March 1939 stated that Czech law remained valid 'except in so far as it contradicts the spirit of the protection undertaken by the German Reich'. The Reichsprotektor could veto Czech laws and judicial decisions which he found objectionable. The Reich government could also 'take measures necessary for the maintenance of law and order'. A system of German courts was established which dealt with all matters involving German citizens. The subordination of Czech to German law implicit in these provisions was extended on 3 April 1939 when the German criminal code was applied to the Protectorate. This brought a whole series of offences, including political dissent, under Nazi jurisdiction and reduced the Czech courts to a secondary role. On 7 June 1939 the Reichsprotektor was empowered to change Czech law in accordance with 'common interests' and reverse the verdicts of Czech courts. New German laws became part of the Protectorate legal code and did not require confirmation by the Czech courts. Moreover with the German occupying forces came the Gestapo which was unhampered by any form of legal restraint. In the next six years the draconian punishments imposed by the German courts and the arbitrary terror of the secret police became the key elements of the Nazi effort to smash the nation and reduce the Czechs to political impotence.

The most powerful German courts in the Protectorate were the so-called 'special courts' established in Bohemia/Moravia as early as 15 March 1939. First set up by the Nazis in 1933 to handle criminal cases without regard for due process, their role was extended with the outbreak of war to cover a whole range of offences relating to the home front. For the Nazis justice was not the goal. The role of the special courts, now renamed 'summary courts of the inner front', was to crush crime and political dissent wherever they appeared. The odds were heavily stacked against the defence. The judges decided what evidence was admissable and there was no appeal against the sentence which was often death or a long spell of imprisonment with hard labour. A Czech brought before such a court was at an additional disadvantage because the only language used was German. The accused was not entitled to a translation. These courts enforced a series of wartime decrees introduced in 1939. The 'Decree on Extraordinary Measures Related to Broadcasting' made it a criminal offence to listen to a foreign radio station. Spreading foreign news was defined as aiding and abetting the enemy and carried a death sentence. The 'Decree on Asocial Elements' imposed draconian punishments for offences such as food hoarding and instituted the death sentence for crimes which took advantage of the blackout or exploited 'the unusual conditions imposed by the war'. The 'Decree on Violent Criminals' made the use of a weapon during a rape, robbery or violent crime, punishable by death. The 'Malicious Offences Law' outlawed political jokes and made 'grumblers, carpers and fault-finders' into criminals.

The summary courts were particularly oppressive in the occupied areas where nearly every offence against the Nazi New Order from forging ration cards and withholding farm animals from slaughter to failing to observe the blackout regulations, was defined as damaging the war effort. The Prague court, consisting of three German judges, sat in a special trial room at Pankrác Prison, with sombre black curtains on every wall. In a typical two-week period in June 1943, it dealt with a variety of offences including over-pricing, hiding a pig, making black-market purchases, over-charging for washing soda, unauthorized slaughter of cattle, milling of grain without a permit, watering milk, withholding eggs, hiding grain, clandestine sales and over-charging for the extermination of rats. In accordance with the Nazi demand that asocial behaviour must be punished particularly severely when the entire nation was 'engaged in a bitter struggle to defend itself against the enemy of the fatherland', the court handed out huge fines and long periods of imprisonment. Those sentenced to death were allowed only ninety seconds to adress the bench before being marched into the adjacent execution room where they were hanged. In April 1944, Karl Hermann Frank boasted that the special courts, acting with 'lightning speed and utmost severity', were killing a hundred Czechs a month.

In December 1944 the Prague special court sentenced a sixty-three-year-old Roman Catholic priest to death for 'malicious remarks'. He had held a mass for a condemned man and spread the rumour that Jews were being tortured at Terezín. The court concluded that : 'Spreaders of political calumnies, who as clergymen find it proper to . . . stab the German Reich in the back when it is engaged in a war . . . deserve no other fate than to be eliminated from their national community.' The priest was guillotined at Pankrác Prison on 16 January 1945. Although no appeals were allowed by the defence, Nazi prosecutors could recall sentences they considered too lenient. On 7 November 1941 two Czech brothers were sentenced to eight and ten years imprisonment by the Prague special court for selling stolen ration coupons. This decision was appealed on behalf of the Reich Chief Prosecutor to the Supreme Court in Leipzig which nullified it and returned the case to Prague with the suggestion that a death sentence should be considered. The judges obliged and the brothers were sent to the gallows.

The Nazi legal system imposed on the Protectorate created a hierarchy based on race with German at the top, Czechs in the middle and Jews at the bottom. Anti-Jewish legislation, modelled on the Nuremberg Laws, was issued by the Reichsprotektor on 21 June 1939 (see Chapter Six). In September 1940, in a case involving a Czech man and a Jewish woman, the Nazi Supreme Court declared that Czechs were covered by Nazi race laws although for other purposes they were not considered citizens of the Reich. This meant that sexual intercourse with a Jew became an offence under the 'Blood Protection Law' of 1935. According to the court, the defendant was 'an inhabitant of the Protectorate of Bohemia and Moravia . . . since the Protectorate belongs to the territory of the Great German Reich, its members enjoy the protection of the Reich, even if they

The execution chamber at Pankrác Prison and the quillotine used by the Nazis

are not ethnic Germans'. In this case 'the protection of the German Reich' meant exemplary punishment for something that was not even a misdemeanour under the Czech criminal code. The special courts were particularly harsh in cases involving race law or where a Jew was accused of a criminal offence. After 1941 it became a crime punishable by death to hide a Jew or to conceal Jewish property. In such cases not only

the offender but also his entire family were executed and all their property was forfeited to the state. In 1942 the courts waived jurisdiction over Jews charged with criminal offences. Henceforth they were to be immediately dealt with by the Gestapo.

In September 1941, when Heydrich arrived in Prague, and again after his assassination in May 1942, martial law tribunals were established to impose summary justice on those accused of disturbing the political or economic stability of the Protectorate. These bodies, which were staffed by the Gestapo, were even more arbitrary and savage than the special courts of the inner front. There was no defence and no hope of an acquittal. The accused were either condemned to death or handed over to the security police to meet an anonymous end. Between 28 September 1941 and 20 January 1942 the Prague martial law court, sitting in the Petschek Palace under SS Sturmbannführer Illmer, handed out 486 death sentences and sent another 2,242 to concentration camps where most of them were murdered. In the new wave of repression after the assassination of Heydrich, the Prague martial law court, this time chaired by the head of the Gestapo in the Protectorate, SS Standartenführer Hans Geschke, sentenced 1,017 people to death between 27 May and 2 July 1942. Under the so-called 'Schnellverfahren' (accelerated proceedings) the accused were not even present during their summary trial. As one Gestapo man later testified : 'No session took place with this court and the proceedings were a formality only, because only names were read, the factual action was brought out in brief and without any further proceedings the verdicts were passed, having been prepared beforehand.' The victims included the entire families of those caught expressing approval of the assassination. It was also this court which on 29 September 1942 sentenced to death 254 members of the families of the parachutists who had carried out the attack on Heydrich and the resistance workers who had helped them. Sentence was carried out on 24 October at Mauthausen concentration camp. The men were shot. The women and children went to the gas chambers.

Important cases of treason or sabotage were tried by the Volksgerichtshof, the Nazi People's Court, which became notorious under Roland Freisler for its treatment of the bomb plotters, the 'July traitors' who attempted to assassinate Hitler in 1944. Even

before Freisler, however, the People's Court was harsh and arbitrary. As one of its prosecutors remarked, its purpose was not to dispense impartial justice but 'to annihilate the enemies of national socialism'. On 20 March 1940 three Czechs were sentenced to death by the People's Court for possession of explosives with intent to damage war industry. In 1944 it also condemned the leader of the clandestine nationalist sports organization, SOKOL, Dr Jan Kellner. The most famous Czech victim of the court, however, was General Alois Eliáš, the Prime Minister of the Protectorate government, who was tried for treason in September 1941. The Gestapo had possessed evidence of Eliáš's contacts with Beneš and the exile movement since 1940 but Hitler was reluctant to authorize action until the crisis in the late summer of 1941 that led to Heydrich's appointment as Acting Reichsprotektor. Heydrich invested the case with symbolic significance. The arrest of Eliáš would bring the Czech government into line and initiate his reign of terror by showing that nobody was beyond the reach of the SS.

Before flying to Prague, Heydrich arranged both the trial and the verdict with Otto Thierack, Freisler's predecessor as President of the People's Court. In the process he brushed aside Thierack's argument that the charges could legally only be brought by the Chief State Prosecutor. As Heydrich remarked: 'I have been given plenipoteniary powers by the Führer, and with this justification I shall order that in this case the charge will be made by the Reichsprotektor.' On 28 September 1941, the day after Heydrich's arrival in Prague, Eliáš was arrested by the Gestapo at his office. On 1 October a special session of the People's Court under Thierack opened at 10:00 in Gestapo headquarters at the Petschek Palace and condemned Eliáš to death within four hours for 'supporting the enemy'. The same day the court sent the Mayor of Prague, Otokar Klapka, who had been in detention since July 1940, to the gallows. Part of the charge against Eliáš was withholding information about Klapka's resistance activities and he was now no longer required. Eliáš, however, was not executed but held as a hostage for the good behaviour of his colleagues. As Heydrich explained, he had arrested only the key man: 'I preferred not to make a clean sweep; that would have left me no one to work with.' Eliáš was finally executed eight months later, on 19 June 1942, a victim of the SS terror that followed the assassination of Heydrich.

Over 2,000 of those condemned by the Nazi courts during the Protectorate were executed by firing squad at Prague-Kobylisy where there were two SS rifle ranges. Executions took place in the evenings between 18:30 and 21:00. The prisoners were brought by truck from Pankrác Prison and held in a house next to the killing ground. From there they were taken out in groups of ten and tied to stakes in front of a wall which was sandbagged to prevent ricochets. A shallow channel behind the posts carried away the blood of the dead. After each volley, the SS officer in charge of the firing squad would take his pistol and shoot any prisoner who still showed signs of life through the head. A squad of white-coated assistants would take away the corpses in stark wooden coffins, sometimes three to a box, and another batch of prisoners would be marched up to the posts.

There was also an execution hall at Pankrác Prison where condemned prisoners were either hanged or guillotined. George Bilainkin, a journalist who visited Pankrác just after the war, described what he saw there in

A memorial to the men and women shot at the Kobylisy execution ground

A poster in Czech and German announcing the execution of prisoners condemned to death by the Prague special court

his diary. Adjacent to the execution chamber was a row of 'last day' cells where the prisoners were held without food or water. Final messages had been scratched on the whitewashed walls. One read : 'My son and I are about to die. Farewell Czechoslovakia.' Another : 'Goodbye my native country. I am about to be hanged.' In the death chamber itself, 'slaughterhouse white tiles rose about six feet, the rest of the walls and the ceiling being spotlessly white. A long iron girder decorated one end of the chamber, and on it were fourteen hooks, of the kind found in modern butchers' shops. Beneath was carefully planed wooden platform, which they removed when man or woman had been attached by rope to hook. Long pole enabled warders to push body and hook along the girder on rollers, so as to make room for other candidates for death. Victims saw hanging bodies before being tied up. Occasionally there was a queue, and for those who had to wait their turn . . . chairs were provided.' There was also a guillotine : 'Former assistant to senior executioner told us that knife over guillotine weighed sixty-five kilos . . . In adjoining corridor were formerly kept men and women destined to die the same day. Sole relief from monotonous wait was merciless refrain of descent of knife. I glanced at books . . . showing how Frank's officials had kept record of all men and women hanged or guillotined. They were books of endless pages, giving endless details.'

The relatives of the accused had to pay for the executions and for the cost of the public posters announcing the sentence. In a final bizarre touch, the debt could be paid off in monthly instalments. As the war drew to an end in 1945 the pace of the executions quickened as the Nazis took revenge on their enemies in a final spasm of terror. Fifty-five men and women were scheduled to die as late as March 1945 when executions were suspended. Five weeks later, the Prague uprising brought an end to German rule. Three British prisoners of war who were held in Pankrác at the time, recalled that around midday the sound of shots was heard around the prison and a bomb hit the bakery. Looking through their tiny barred window, they could see the surrounding apartment blocks, which were inhabited by German officials, silent and shuttered. After a period of quiet, firing began again late in the afternoon and jets screamed low across the building. The prisoners began a riot, yelling and banging on the doors of their cells : 'We shouted to our neighbours to behave themselves – that the Germans were still apparently in control of the city – but they paid no attention . . . Then there were keys turning in the locks and the Czech guards shortly set everyone free. We rushed

The detention cells in the basement of the Gestapo headquarters

to the commissary and got some bread, first thing. I had a loaf of four hundred grams as the three of us walked through the gates free at last.' The SS had fled from the prison early that afternoon, abandoning their condemned victims : 'Men and women who had written their farewell messages while waiting, on chairs, to be taken to the iron girder for dispatch, had survived.'

If the courts were one aspect of the terror, the other was the SS security police, SIPO, which included the criminal police or Kripo, the secret political police, the Gestapo, and the SS intelligence service, the Sicherheitsdienst or SD. There were three security police commanders (Befehlshaber der Sicherheitspolizei/BdS) during the Protectorate. The first was SS Oberführer Walther Stahlecker who left Prague in 1940 to become BdS in Oslo. The following year he was made head of one of Heydrich's murder commandos in Russia, Einsatzgruppe A, which massacred thousands of Jews caught behind the German lines in the East. Stahlecker was ambushed and fatally wounded by Soviet partisans and died in the hospital train taking him back to Germany on 23 March 1942. Heydrich arranged an elaborate funeral service in the 'German Hall' at the Hradčany Castle for this mass killer. The Prague Philharmonic Orchestra played Schubert's *Unfinished Symphony* and Heydrich gave a short oration, praising Stahlecker as a true SS man who had fallen in battle with the Bolshevik enemy. In the first courtyard an SS guard of honour fired three volleys over the coffin which was then carried at a slow march through the streets of Prague where the flags flew at half mast. Stahlecker's successor in Prague was SS Standartenführer Horst Böhme, a thirty-three-year-old thug who had joined the SS in 1930.

Böhme, described by his superiors as 'a faultless national socialist', came to Prague from the killing grounds of White Russia where he had headed Einsatzgruppe B and served as BdS of the occupied Ukraine. He was a flamboyant character who roared around Prague in an open red Tatra sports car. A man of savage temper, he once felled a Prague hotel porter with a telephone for insolence. His victim was then arrested and sent to a concentration camp. Already a mass murderer when he arrived in Prague, it was Böhme who first proposed Lidice as the target of Nazi reprisals for the assassination of Heydrich, a suggestion Hitler acted upon on the evening of Heydrich's funeral. The last BdS was SS Standartenführer Dr Erwin Weinmann, another young Nazi on the make, who was transferred to Prague in March 1943 from Gestapo headquarters in Berlin. Weinmann vanished during the Prague uprising and was assumed dead by a German court in 1947.

The room known as 'the cinema' where prisoners of the Gestapo awaited interrogation

The most powerful element in the security police was the Gestapo which arrived in Prague with the German army on 15 March 1945 as part of a special action group under SS Standartenführer O. E. Rasch. Its first task codenamed Operation Gitter (see Chapter One) was to secure important Czech intelligence archives and to arrange the round-up of known anti-Nazis. Rasch's activities were supervised by the head of the Gestapo, Heinrich 'Gestapo' Müller, who established himself in the opulent surroundings of the Palace Hotel on Herrengasse. At the beginning of May 1939 a permanent headquarters was established at the Petschek Palace on Bredauer Street, a former bank building belonging to a Jewish financier and coal magnate who had sold his holdings to the Czech government after Munich and emigrated to Britain. Behind the Nazi flags which covered the front of the building, the Gestapo established a vast complex of laboratories, offices and torture chambers. In the basement a series of holding cells was built for prisoners under interrogation. One of them was used to store crude wooden coffins for those who died under 'rigorous interrogation'. Nearly 1000 people worked in this 'palace of death', the majority auxiliary staff, filing clerks, women typists and translators, who were either German speaking Czechs or Sudeten Germans.

The Petschek Palace was a place of terror even for those who had not been arrested. Sir Paul Dukes visited the building in July 1939 when he was trying to trace a missing Czech refugee. He later recalled that it required all his 'reserves of cheerfulness to withstand the chilling atmosphere of that sinister establishment. Its high hall and corridors seemed dark even on a summer afternoon. Perhaps it was the sombre figures of the Black Guards that made them appear so. These, whose task was to act as wardens and guides, stood about on the steps and in the vestibule looking like jailers.' If this was the reaction of a British subject, protected by his passport and his reputation as a ferocious anti-Communist, the impact on suspects brought to the Petschek Palace for interrogation can be imagined. The whole process was designed by the Gestapo to induce a feeling of helplessness and fear. Prisoners were driven in cars or vans into an interior courtyard and hustled downstairs to 'the cinema', a blank walled room with long wooden benches. There they had to wait in utter silence, watched by a Gestapo guard. Any movement or attempt to talk brought three days solitary confinement without food or water. The aim was to break the victims psychologically before interrogation began. They were meant to imagine what could happen to them at the hands of the Gestapo. The room was known as 'the cinema', because in their imagination, the prisoners projected terrible images on to the bare walls. On the ground floor, facing the inner courtyard, was a small torture room with a double wall to muffle the screams of those under interrogation. Various forms of torture were employed, from routine beating and kicking to the use of thumbscrews and other bone-crushing instruments. Some prisoners were tied to the central heating pipes and suffered severe burns. Others were bound by their arms and legs to a pole suspended between two tables and beaten with clubs.

The Prague Gestapo had branch offices throughout Bohemia/Moravia. The head of this system of institutionalized terror was SS Standardtenführer Dr Hans Ulrich Geschke. Aged thirty-seven in 1939, Geschke was one of the bright young men attracted to the SS by the prospects of speedy promotion and its image as an Ayran élite. A law graduate of the best universities, Berlin, Tübingen and Göttingen, Geschke had joined the Nazi party in January 1932. He became an attorney in Hanover and acted as legal adviser to the local party before joining the Gestapo in Dortmund in November 1934. Geschke liked to pretend that he was a gentleman, but the educated façade hid the reality of a cold, bureaucratic killer. Beneath Geschke, the Gestapo was divided into several divisions. Section II(A) dealt with Communism, Anarchism and Trotskyism. It was headed by Willi Leimer, 'one of the most intelligent, brutal and astute officers in Prague'. Section II (BM) was concerned with political resistance, crimes against German nationals and anything relating to the cinema and theatre. It was headed by two officers called Kruppke and Glesagen. Section II (C) covered German anti-Nazis. Section II (D) kept prisoners' file cards. Section II (E) covered black-market offences. Section II (F) kept the archives. Section II (G) handled protection of important figures, sabotage, illegal weapons,

SS Standartenführer Dr Hans Ulrich Geschke, Head of the Prague Gestapo in the first half of the war

and assaults on party or state officials. It was headed by Heinz von Pannwitz, a career police officer. Pannwitz also controlled Section II (H) which investigated corruption in state and party. In May 1942 he was put in charge of the special commission that investigated the assassination of Heydrich. Section II (I) under Schulz was concerned with counter-intelligence. The criminal police, or Kripo, under SS Obersturmbannführer Friederich Sowa, shared the Petschek Palace, but had its own bureaucratic structure. Relations between the two branches were cool and Sowa's deputy, August Lyss, was not even a member of the Nazi party. The Kripo dealt with ordinary, or non-political crime, involving Reich Germans.

While the upper ranks of the Prague Gestapo were staffed by university graduates or career policemen, the agents at the bottom were often political gangsters of the worst kind. Sir Paul Dukes met one in July 1939 during his search for the missing Czech refugee. The Gestapo man was an 'individual of the shadiest type. I saw pretty clearly how things were for I had experience of such types in the [Soviet] Cheka-OGPU. They were always ill-paid underlings and petty officials who could be bought and were very useful for odd jobs.' It transpired that the man was selling false passports and exit visas using contacts in the Prague criminal underworld. According to Dukes, there had 'already been one big corruption scandal at the Prague Gestapo at the end of March . . . when some officials had even been shot and others dismissed'. Many agents were still in business, smuggling foreign currency and precious stones into Switzerland using official couriers whose baggage was never checked by the customs or the border police. Corruption continued throughout the war. Two Gestapo agents, Iser and Gall, were arrested in 1941 for accepting bribes from the families of political prisoners. A member of Pannwitz's anti-corruption section committed suicide the following year when he was found guilty of extortion. Jewish property provided a particularly lucrative source of income and most of those involved were never caught.

The Gestapo was a small force. There were only 2000 SIPO agents (Gestapo, Kripo and SD) in the entire Protectorate. In Prague itself the Kripo numbered 250, the Gestapo 150. As in Germany the secret police relied on a widespread informer system to facilitate its work. A Nazi official once sneered that the Czechs were a 'nation of denouncers and whores. If we locked up everybody who gave us information there wouldn't be enough prisons to hold them.' Some informers were members of Vlajka (Flag), an extremist party modelled on the Nazis, who acted from conviction, while others were professionals who worked for money. Amongst the most notorious was Nestor Holejko, a Ukrainian who was responsible for the death of at least 29 members of the resistance. Another was

Jaroslav Nachtmann, a former Czech policeman of German extraction. Posing as a member of Soviet intelligence, Nachtmann penetrated several Communist networks and even presided at meetings of party cells. Many informers were criminals who had always made money by selling information to the police. Sir Paul Dukes met someone of this type in a Prague pub shortly after the occupation began : 'I felt sure this man was what the Germans would call a "Kleiner Schieber", a sort of petty sharper, the kind of fellow who might act as a receiver of stolen goods or swindler's go-between. He might seek to justify his conspirative dealings with the Gestapo to his own people on patriotic grounds as undermining German authority when really the only motive was their lucrativeness.' Paid informers were supplemented by people blackmailed into working for the police. They included suspects who had been 'turned' by the Gestapo and the families of prisoners who cooperated to save a relative from the gallows, the guillotine or the firing squad.

The Gestapo also relied heavily on malicious denunciations. Nearly 25 per cent of cases stemmed from this source. Every day anonymous letters arrived at the Petschek Palace : X had a radio tuned to the BBC or Moscow. Y was hoarding food. Z had told a political joke. According to Pannwitz, after the assassination of Heydrich the Gestapo was innundated with denunciations accusing neighbours of harbouring the parachutists or of expressing approval of the attack. The Gestapo also targeted groups and individuals suspected of sympathizing with the resistance or the exile movement – members of the banned SOKOL, former army officers, families of exiles. They would be approached by agents posing as parachutists from Britain or Russia who would ask for help. A positive response meant arrest and execution. In 1944 Molča Dvořák, the manager of a Prague export firm involved with the Communist underground, was betrayed by a 'Soviet agent who was in fact working for the Gestapo. Captured parachutists and former members of the resistance were often used for such unsavoury tasks. One of the most prominent was Karel Čurda of OUT DISTANCE, dropped into the Protectorate by a British aircraft in March 1942. It was Čurda who betrayed the assassins of Heydrich and he spent the remainder of the war as a Gestapo agent. Another was Václav Kindl of INTRANSITIVE. Captured in March 1943, Kindl worked for the Germans until he was shot dead in error during a Gestapo operation he was assisting in May 1944. Informing and infiltration became so common that the resistance found it very hard to organize. Nobody was prepared to trust a stranger or to take unnecessary risks.

A victim of the Prague Gestapo

This reluctance was reinforced by the doctrine of collective responsibility. The Gestapo arrested and killed the families of captured resistance workers. In June 1942 two entire communities, Lidice and Ležáky, were wiped out in the terror that followed the death of Heydrich. In February 1940, managers and foremen in the armaments industry were made answerable for the security of their factories. Each had to sign a document stating: 'Today I have been warned by the Armament Inspector... that I bear personal responsibility, with all its consequences, for the prevention of acts of sabotage in my plant.' This approach was intended to make the Czechs police themselves, motivated by the fear of retribution if they failed to denounce subversive elements. It was brutally effective. The first Czech parachutists dropped from Britain in December 1941 were stunned by the difficulties of living underground and the unwillingness of most ordinary people to help them. But the caution of the population was understandable. As Professor Vladimír Vondráček, a Prague psychiatrist, later recalled, nobody who had not lived through the period could understand the numbing shock of being told by a janitor or neighbour: 'The Gestapo is looking for you.' By the middle of the war people flinched at the sound of a car stopping in front of their apartment or an unexpected ring on their doorbell, fearing a police raid caused by an anonymous denunciation.

The Gestapo also took hostages who could be executed in reprisal for resistance activity. In October 1942, after the death of Heydrich, relatives of the exiles were detained in a special camp. Announcing the news at a Nazi rally in Prague, Frank remarked: 'We did it to shut the mouths of the speakers from London... Should they go on intriguing we shall be compelled to take appropriate measures against the prisoners.' The following year there was a round-up of 'political friends of Dr Beneš' who were sent to concentration camps 'without prejudice to severer measures which may be taken'. In January 1943, Böhme ordered the compilation of a register of individuals who could be murdered in retaliation for acts of sabotage. The list was to include 'politically incriminated persons', 'relatives of emigrants' and 'Jewish half-breeds' of Czech origin. Relatives of earlier Gestapo victims were also to be included 'because they must be presumed to be [our] enemies'.

The Gestapo was backed up by another force, the uniformed police or Ordnungspolizei. There were 10 police battalions totalling 5000 men in the Protectorate, headed by a Befehlshaber der Ordnungspolizei (BdO) with his headquarters at 14 General Roettig

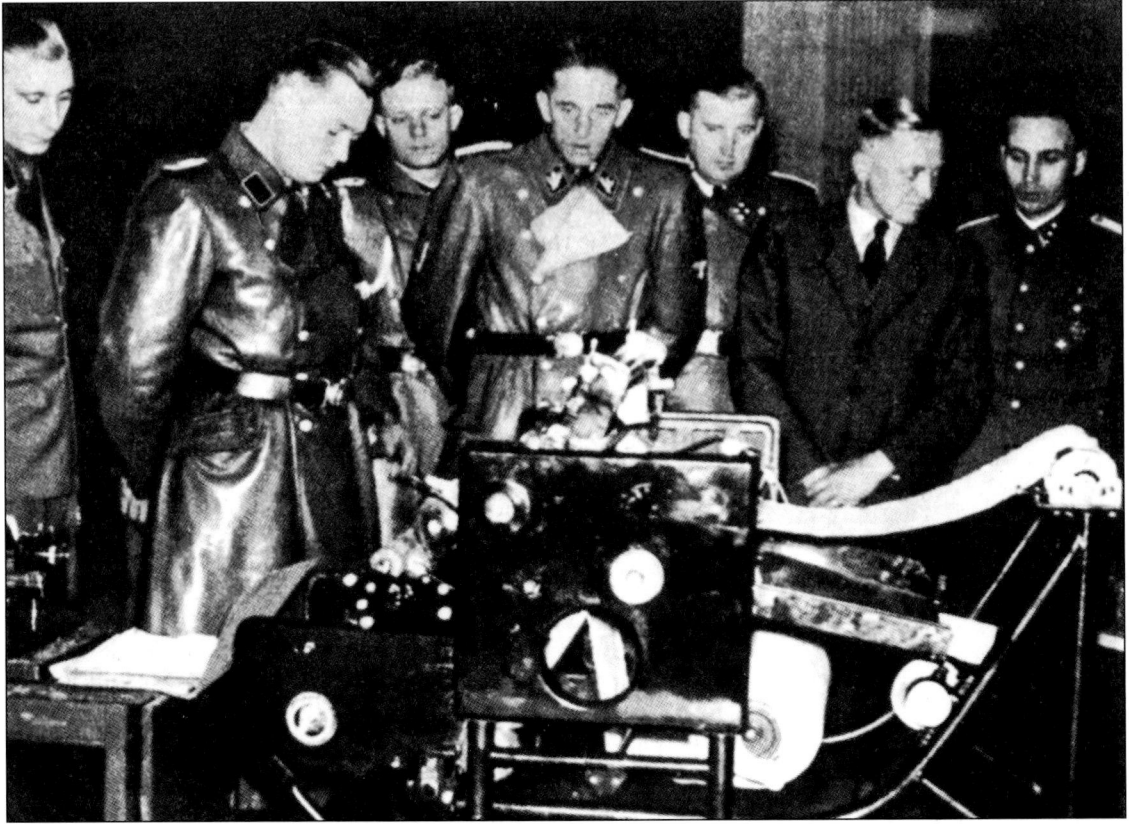

Horst Böhme (in leather coat) and K. H. Frank (in the centre) inspecting an illegal printing press uncovered by the Prague Gestapo

Strasse in Prague-Bubeneč. The Ordnungspolizei was a military force with its own transport, machine-guns and communications system. Composed of young volunteers and older reservists, it was employed by Himmler for special tasks behind the front, including the massacre of Polish and Russian Jews. In Prague, the Ordnungspolizei acted as riot police during the student demonstrations of November 1939 when it gained a reputation for brutality. In May 1945 it was again sent into the streets when Frank attempted to suppress the Prague uprising. The uniformed police provided the firing squads at Kobylisy and the guards for the deportation trains that took the Jews to Terezín. An Ordnungspolizei company of two NCOs and twenty men under SS Hauptsturmführer Max Rostock was responsible for the cold-blooded murder of 173 men from Lidice on 10 June 1942. The prisoners were shot in groups of ten against an orchard wall which was covered with mattresses to prevent ricochets. The later victims had to step over the bodies of their friends and relatives as they were led out for execution. After the first fifty had been killed, three policemen had to be replaced. The others were issued with schnapps to steady their nerves and by the end of the day most of them were hopelessly drunk.

The commanders of the Ordnungspolizei were never important in the politics of the Protectorate. They were usually men with a military or police background absorbed into the SS in the late 1930s as part of Himmler's attempt to merge SS and police into a 'state protection corps'. The first, Lieutenant-General von Kamptz, was a former soldier who had headed the uniformed police in Berlin before his transfer to Prague in March 1939. SS Gruppenführer Ernst Hitzegrad, appointed in 1943, had served with the uniformed police since 1919 and came to Prague from Dresden. He was condemned to death by the Czechs after the war but the sentence was commuted and he was finally released in 1961. His successor, the last Ordnungspolizei commander, was SS Brigadeführer Paul Geibel, a former naval officer and insurance salesman, who had joined the police in 1935. Although a party member since 1931, he had not joined the SS until 1938. Geibel spent most of the war in Poland and was transferred to Prague in February 1945 because of his experience as head of a police battle group in Warsaw during the uprising. Captured by the Czechs in 1945, he was returned to Warsaw and spent many years in a Polish prison. The Ordnungspolizei was despised by the Gestapo which considered it second-rate, a reflexion of the rivalry between the uniformed and plain-clothes branches of many police forces.

The Czech police continued to operate under the close supervision of the Nazis. It was used to tackle ordinary crimes, like burglary and prostitution, which the Gestapo lacked the local knowledge, language and manpower to control. The Kripo even arranged courses for Czech detectives on modern forensic methods and fingerprinting. Any case involving a Reich citizen, or with a political dimension, however, had to be handed over to the Kripo or Gestapo. The Czech uniformed police was employed on traditional traffic and beat duties. It was also mobilized to provide extra manpower in big security operations like the massive house-to-house search that followed the assassination of Heydrich in May 1942. On these occasions some policemen took a risk and allowed suspects to slip through the net. According to Walther Schellenberg, who accompanied Himmler and Heydrich during the Nazi march into Prague, the Reichsführer SS was impressed by the Czech police who lined the streets and talked about recruiting them into the Waffen SS. But this never happened. Neither Hitler nor Karl Hermann Frank had forgotten the mass desertion of Czech troops from the Habsburg Army to the Russians in the First World War and did not intend to take a similar risk during the Second.

The Czech criminal police was placed under the supervision of the Kripo chief, Friedrich Sowa. A special section of the Prague Police Presidium, Presidium B, headed by Inspector Jaroslav Ženatý, was responsible for translating reports of incidents involving Germans from the ten district police stations and passing the cases over to the Kripo. Ženatý had served in the Sudetenland before Munich and was appointed to Presidium B because of his fluent German. Despite Schellenberg's claim, the SS never trusted the Czech police. Shortly after the beginning of the occupation, four policemen were arrested on trumped-up charges and shot at Prague-Kobylisy. Leading Czech police officers were forced to witness the execution which was clearly intended as a warning to others of the consequences of resistance. Thereafter the police was regularly purged. In 1940 a branch of the underground group

An Ordnungspolizei patrol in the streets of Prague's Little Quarter

Obrana Národa was discovered by the Gestapo in the police presidium. The officers involved were tortured and killed. Under Heydrich a campaign was launched against policemen who had tolerated 'illegal gambling' and hoarded rationed food. This camouflaged a new search for resistance cells. At the same time Heydrich attempted to reward collaboration. Policemen involved in fights with parachutists or the underground were given rewards and presented with special pistols by the Reichsprotektor. The widows of policemen killed during such operations were given fat German pensions. Despite six years of infiltration and supervision, however, it was the police that provided the main force behind the Prague uprising in May 1945.

Secret resistance cells emerged in the police at the very beginning of the occupation. In March 1939 the Gestapo set up a special office in the Czech Criminal Investigation Department to process the exit visas of people who wanted to flee the Protectorate. The Czech inspectors assigned to this task bent the rules and allowed hundreds of Czechs and Czech Jews to escape abroad, where many of them joined the army in exile. The Gestapo eventually discovered what was going on and closed the division in early 1940. Several policemen were executed. In the autumn of 1939, the Gestapo asked for fourteen German-speaking detectives to act as translators to Sections II (A), II (BM) and III, which dealt with Communist and non-Communist resistance and counter-espionage. Most of these men were anti-Nazis and did not go willingly. Their work at the Petschek Palace gave them access to Gestapo secrets which they passed on to a resistance group codenamed Blaník, founded by forty detectives and uniformed officers in 1940. A leading member of Blaník was the head of Presidium B, Inspector Jaroslav Ženatý. He had to take a report on criminal activity in the city to the Petschek Palace every week and used the opportunity to pick up knowledge

The so-called 'Small Fortress' at Terezin, used by the Gestapo as a detention centre for political prisoners

useful to the resistance. Blaník even had a German collaborator in Section II (D) of the Gestapo which kept prisoners' file cards. From these sources it learned the names of resistance workers under surveillance by the Germans, what had been revealed by those who were detained and even the names of parachutists from Britain who had been 'turned' by the Gestapo.

This information was passed on to Dr Strnad, a former aide to President Beneš, who still worked at the Hradčany and by him to ÚVOD, the Central Council of the Home Resistance, for transmission to London. Another line of communication was established through a sympathetic Swiss diplomat in Prague, codenamed René, who took out a long report when he was transferred to Zurich in the autumn of 1942. Blaník also had contacts with the Communist underground through Molča Dvořák, the manager of a Prague export company, whose wife was a courier for the party. Thanks to the Czech inspectors working for Section II (A), the police ring was sometimes able to give the Communists advance warning of Gestapo raids and news of what arrested party members had revealed under interrogation. As Ženatý recalled, some policemen also tried to protect ordinary citizens against denunciations which were often filed with the Police Praesidium rather than the Gestapo. Those accused of insulting the Reich or the occupying forces would be charged under a Czech statute for 'breach of public order' and sentenced to a few weeks in prison. A similar complaint filed with Section II (BM) of the Gestapo meant a hearing before a special court and a possible death sentence. Since this part of the Gestapo was staffed 'by agents of no particular intelligence or talent who lacked the will to pursue such small fry', this tactic often worked even where a duplicate complaint had been laid at the Petschek Palace. Some complaints were always passed on to the Germans. Amongst the most common were cases in which Czech petty criminals posed as Gestapo men for the purposes of blackmail or to extort protection money from shops and pubs.

Dr Ženatý recalled one particular case in which he was able to minimize the damage caused by informers. In October 1940 two of the staff at the National Theatre claimed that several members of the chorus and orchestra had made derogatory remarks about the Reich. The report was probably fuelled by professional jealousy but it was too important not to forward to the Gestapo which would inevitably arrest the accused and close the theatre, a seat of Czech culture for over 100 years. Ženatý knew, however, from the film star Lída Baarová that the Nazi Propaganda Minister Joseph Goebbels was about to visit the city, information that had been withheld from the Czechs for security reasons.

Dr Jaroslav Ženatý, of the Prague Criminal Police, who was a liaison officer with the Prague Gestapo before his own arrest by the Nazis. He spent the rest of the war in the 'Small Fortress' at Terezín

Baarová, a former lover of Goebbels, had been told about the trip in advance. Ženatý went to the theatre and arranged a counter-denunciation by the rest of the staff who signed a document stating that the two informants were jealous trouble-makers who had acted out of malice. He then passed the entire file on to the Gestapo knowing that nobody at the Petschek Palace would have the nerve to arrest the entire cast on the eve of an important visit during which Goebbels was scheduled to see them perform Smetana's opera *The Bartered Bride*.

Ženatý's gamble succeeded and the Gestapo dismissed the incident rather than risk a row with the powerful Propaganda Minister. Goebbels duly visited the theatre on 7 November 1940 and noted his appreciation in his diary : 'At the National Opera. A very beautiful but shabby building. *Bartered Bride*. Beautifully sung and acted. Under a wonderful conductor.' He had no idea of what had been going on behind the scenes. Shortly afterwards Ženatý learned from a Czech interpreter at the Petschek Palace that Glesgen, Chief of the Gestapo Film and Theatre Section, had remarked : 'Dr Ženatý, that cunning fox, one day we'll get him.' His luck did indeed finally run out like that of so many members of the resistance. Ženatý was detained and questioned several times by the Gestapo before the final destruction of the Blaník group in April 1943, four months after its contact with ÚVOD, Dr Strnad, had been arrested and beheaded. Ženatý was sentenced to death but was then held as a hostage in the 'Small Fortress' at Terezín for the rest of the war. He survived to play a role in the final liberation of Prague.

The uprising of 5 May 1945 took the Gestapo by surprise. One group, under Geschke's successor, Obersturmbannführer Gerke, escaped on the first day, walking down the main railway line to safety. Another 700 agents and collaborators barricaded themselves in the Petschek Palace under Kriminalkommisar Jantur. The building was equipped with strong walls and steel shutters proof against anything except tanks or heavy artillery, which the Czechs did not possess. Jaroslav Ženatý, released from the 'Small Fortress' as part of Frank's abortive plan to install a transitional government composed of arrested underground leaders (see Chapter Seven), telephoned Jantur from the Police Presidium on Bartolomäeusgasse and asked him to surrender, promising that if his men left the archives intact and came out of the building unarmed, they would be treated as prisoners of war. Jantur refused and the Czechs decided to surround the Petschek Palace and await the arrival of the American or Soviet armies. On 8 May, however, a ceasefire was negotiated which allowed all German forces to withdraw from Prague unharmed. As part of this deal the remaining Gestapo agents were able to slip away by car and truck, taking some of their papers with them. For the Czechs it was the end of six years of institutionalized terror based on the gallows, the guillotine and the secret police. As the war ended, there were apartments all over Prague where there was 'no news of the principal tenant, the man the Nazis dragged out of bed in the middle of the night and took for a lingering death in a concentration

The Nazi Propaganda Minister Joseph Goebbels arriving in Prague in November 1940

Z NÁVŠTĚVY Dr. JOSEFA GOEBBELSE V PRAZE

Pan říšský ministr propagandy a lidové osvěty Dr. J. Goebbels v rozmluvě s p. státním presidentem Dr. Emilem Háchou na Hradě pražském.

Na koncertě Berlínské filharmonie v Deutsches Opernhaus v Praze. Zprava: Pan říš. protektor svobodný pán von Neurath, pan říš. ministr Dr. J. Goebbels, svob. paní von Neurath a pan stát. president Dr. E. Hácha

V Národním divadle na slavnostním představení Smetanovy »Prodané nevěsty«.
Foto (5): Centropress, Praha.

Z návštěvy ve filmových ateliérech na Barrandově. Zprava: Pan státní sekretář S. S. Gruppenführer K. H. Frank, pan říš. protektor von Neurath a pan říš. ministr Dr. J. Goebbels.

Při projevu NSDAP k německým soukmenovcům v Průmyslovém paláci.

A page from a popular Czech magazine showing highlights from Goebbels' visit to Prague

camp or for summary execution in prison, because of his political activity or thanks to the spite of a Czech collaborator'.

Between 1939 and 1945 the Protectorate was a true police state. Amongst all the occupied peoples, only the Czechs had the misfortune to be directly ruled by the SS police apparatus, first under Heydrich, the head of the Nazi security service and then under Daluege, the head of the uniformed police. Before and after their terms of office as acting Reichsprotektor, continuity was provided by Karl Hermann Frank, the State Secretary and Höhere SS und Polizei Führer. As Frank emphasized in April 1944, 'one institution in this area with an alien population has proved to be excellent. It is the personal union between the supreme state leadership and the Higher SS and Police Chief. This personal union is of outstanding political value, because the highest German political and administrative authority simultaneously has at its disposal all the executive forces of the security police, the regular police and the entire Czech police ... as well as field units of the Waffen SS ... It always has at its disposal the SD as its own intelligence instrument.' With this formidable array of forces under his 'central command' he could remain in 'full control of the situation under all circumstances'.

The SS police system aimed at the 'atomization of everyday life', smashing the traditional bonds of civil society and creating a climate of fear and distrust. Czechs were to be turned against each other while their labour was mobilized for the good of their oppressors. Heydrich emphasized in October 1941 that the goal was depoliticization, in which people would put their own personal survival before the wider concerns of nation or community. The evidence suggests that the special courts and the Gestapo achieved this aim. As the experienced observer, Sir Paul Dukes, remarked in July 1939, within months of the occupation: 'I have seen a good deal of life under political terror, first under Bolshevik and latterly under Nazi rule; and I say that no man must be lightly condemned for frailty of character in the conditions of ever-looming persecution and danger in which the unhappy victims of these regimes are forced to dwell, for nerves of steel are needed to withstand them.' As elsewhere in occupied Europe, resistance was never a serious threat to Nazi rule until the allied armies were close enough to save the community from the grim consequences of open rebellion. Both resisters and open collaborators were in a minority. The majority kept their heads down and waited for liberation. Survival of self and family was the aim, not heroic gestures that threatened the safety of the entire community and did little to hasten the end of the war. In this regard the SS terror that followed the assassination of Heydrich was of particular importance, implying that open resistance could mean the decimation of the entire nation. In the postwar period the Communists exploited the social, institutional and psychological breakdown engineered by the SS to promote their own totalitarian regime, based on 'class justice', which excluded certain social groups from the equal protection of the law, and created an omnipresent secret police unrestrained by the courts. Ironically the informer network which underpinned this system was inherited from the Gestapo.

'The Jews from Bohemia and Moravia will be concentrated for evacuation ... in one transit camp. For this purpose Theresienstadt has been completely evacuated by all units of the army ... The Czechs have been advised to move somewhere else ... 50,000 to 60,000 Jews can easily be housed in Theresienstadt ... From there the Jews will be taken to the East'

SS OBERGRUPPENFÜHRER REINHARD HEYDRICH,
2 OCTOBER 1941

CHAPTER FIVE

The Prague Jews

The Old New Synagogue and the Old Jewish Town Hall

A sign proclaims: 'No entry for Jews!'

BEFORE the Munich conference of 1938 destroyed the First Republic, the position of the Czech Jews seemed to be secure. Although popular anti-Semitism existed, particularly in Slovakia and Ruthenia, and there were few Jews in the civil service or the army officer corps, official policy emphasized tolerance. As early as 1900, Masaryk had denounced the conviction of Leopold Hilsner, the 'Czech Dreyfus', on a charge of ritual murder and during the independence struggle he had cultivated Jewish support, particularly in America. This approach continued in the new state founded by Masaryk and Beneš in 1918. From the Jewish point of view Czechoslovakia thus provided by far the most favourable environment in Eastern Europe when compared with the situation in Poland, Rumania and Hungary. The Jewish community of Bohemia/Moravia was largely professional, middle class and urban. Although Zionism had some impact, the Jewish community was integrated, speaking Czech and sending its children to Czech schools. Intermarriage was relatively common. In 1931, thirty-two out of every 100 Jewish grooms married Gentiles. The census of 1930 showed that almost 50 per cent of the Jews in Bohemia/Moravia lived in Prague where they made up 4.17 per cent of the population. Another 25 per cent lived in Brno. Despite a declining birth rate, the Jewish population of Prague was swollen after 1933 by refugees from Nazi persecution in Germany. A variety of organizations, containing both Jews and Gentiles, emerged to provide for the welfare of these newcomers. The city also became a transit point for Jews awaiting entry visas to Britain and the United States. This refugee influx was encouraged by Czechoslovakia's geographical position and the relatively liberal immigration policy pursued by the government until 1937.

After the Munich conference and the collapse of the Masaryk tradition, the position of the Jews began to deteriorate. The new government was under great pressure from Germany to introduce anti-Jewish legislation on the pattern of the Nazi Nuremberg Laws.

On the first day of the Nazi Occupation, Jewish refugees seek asylum in the courtyard of the British Embassy in Thunovská Street

At the same time there was a growth of anti-Semitism in the Czech lands, aimed primarily at German-speaking Jewish refugees. The national sports organization, SOKOL, demanded the expulsion of all those who had arrived since 1918, the so-called 'foreign' Jews. The legal profession called for the exclusion of German-speaking Jews and limits on the numbers of Czech Jewish lawyers allowed to practise. Some hospital boards and insurance companies began to discriminate against Jewish doctors. The German community in the Czech lands, which became almost autonomous after Munich, conducted its own campaign. The press secretary of the German embassy, Freiherr von Gregory, coordinated the dismissal of Jews from all

German theatres and newspapers. Forty-five Jewish professors were fired by the German University in Prague, a notorious hotbed of Nazi subversion.

The government responded to these domestic and foreign demands by limiting immigration from the Sudetenland, now ceded to Nazi Germany. Jews expelled by the new German masters were refused entry into Czechoslovakia and left to eke out a miserable existence along the border. Those who did manage to flee found it almost impossible to obtain work permits. In January 1939 the government announced that it was reviewing the cases of all aliens naturalized since 1918. Although this measure did not affect the established Czech Jewish community, it was a symbol of what was to come. At the same time a small number of civil servants with two Jewish parents were pensioned off as a sop to Berlin. But the regime was unenthusiastic about further measures and outside the ranks of the tiny extremist party, Vlajka, there was little popular support for a radical attack on the Jews. According to the American diplomat, Wilbur Carr, the German demand for anti-Semitic measures had 'met with stubborn resistance from a good part of the population' and President Hácha 'whose daughter was married to a Jew' was said to be exercising a moderating influence. As for the Jewish community, there was an increase in emigration after Munich and, particularly amongst the young, a greater interest in Zionism. But most of the emigrants were refugees from Germany. Despite the looming Nazi threat, few Czech Jews were willing to uproot themselves from the land in which they had lived for generations.

When the Nazis occupied Bohemia/Moravia in March 1939 there were 56,000 Jews in Prague of whom 15,000 were German refugees. Some of the German Jews were swept up in Aktion Gitter (see Chapter One) and taken to concentration camps in the Reich. But apart from a bomb attack on the Old/New Synagogue on 20 March, there was no public reign of terror against the Jews of the capital such as had marked the Nazi occupation of Vienna the previous year. Europe was still at peace and the Germans were conscious of world opinion. While there were anti-Jewish outbreaks in provincial towns with large German populations, in Prague open rabble rousing was left up to the Czech anti-Semites. The aim in this period was to create a climate of prejudice as a preliminary to segregation and forced emigration. The activities of all Jewish

Jewish property and religious objects were confiscated by the Nazis

organizations were immediately banned. In an attempt to promote popular anti-Semitism the Gestapo organized an exhibition entitled 'The Jews as the Enemy of Humanity' which revived stories of ritual murder. Delegations of schoolchildren and workers were compelled to visit this display. At the same time the Czech police were ordered to reopen all unsolved cases involving missing women or children. The rabidly anti-Semitic newspaper, *Der Stürmer,* edited by Julius Streicher, the Gauleiter of Franconia, was displayed to the public on special stands. Meanwhile the Czech government began to draft anti-Jewish legislation along the lines of the Nuremberg Laws and issued an ordinance installing Czech trustees in Jewish businesses. But the first measure was not considered radical enough and the second was an obvious attempt to keep Jewish property out of German hands. On the Jewish question, the Nazis were determined to impose their own solutions.

On 21 June 1939 Neurath issued a decree excluding Jews from the economic life of the Protectorate and forcing them to register their assets. Jewish companies were to be taken over by German 'Treuhänder' (trustees) who would supervise their sale or 'aryanization'. The definition of a Jewish company was a wide one and included businesses considered to be under 'the decisive influence of Jews'. Since the assets of Jews and non-Jews were widely linked, Neurath had created a looters' charter. The decree took the Protectorate government by surprise for it had not even been consulted. The first Hácha's ministers knew about the ordinance was when they read the text in the German press. This measure was the preliminary to forced emigration. The day after the publication of Neurath's decree, the SS 'Jewish expert', Adolf Eichmann, arrived in Prague, establishing himself in a confiscated Jewish villa in Střešovice. Eichmann headed the Zentralstelle für jüdische Auswanderung (The Central Office for Jewish Emigration), an SS bureaucracy for robbing and expelling Jews which had begun work in Vienna the year before. Eichmann's permanent representative in Prague was SS Hauptsturmführer (Captain) Hans Gunther. Although a decree by the Reichsprotektor of 21 July 1939 subordinated Gunther to the security police commander of the Protectorate, SS Brigadeführer (Major General) Walther Stahlecker, he was in fact solely answerable to Eichmann's headquarters.

A central Jewish authority was promoted to facilitate the operations of Gunther's Zentralle. In March 1940 the Jewish communities of the Protectorate were subordinated to the Jewish Religious Council of Prague headed by Dr Emil Kafka and his deputy, Jakub Edelstein, which had been created in the wake of the Nazi occupation. This organization was now expected to register the Jewish population of Bohemia/Moravia and raise funds for emigration. At a meeting with Dr Kafka in the summer of 1939, Eichmann demanded the expulsion of 70,000 Jews within a year. When Kafka protested that there was no money for such a massive undertaking, Eichmann threatened to clear Prague street

by street, sending 300 a day to the concentration camp at Dachau where 'they would become very keen on emigration'. In August 1939 he issued orders for all Jews to resettle in Prague within a year, although this move was never fully implemented. At the same time the Protectorate government began issuing its own restrictions on Jewish citizens. In August 1939 Jews were segregated in Prague restaurants and prohibited from using public baths and swimming pools. It became an offence for Jews to enter such banned areas. But worse was to come. Before the war Czech Jews enjoyed the slender protection of international opinion. Hitler wanted to maintain at least an appearance of respectability to encourage new acts of appeasement by Britain and France. After

The loot was brought to Prague for sorting

September 1939, however, Nazi policy became increasingly radical. The invasion of Poland was the signal for a new series of anti-Jewish measures. On the eve of war prominent members of the Jewish community were rounded up by the Gestapo as part of Operation Albrecht (see Chapter Two) and sent to Dachau where they were held as hostages for the good behaviour of their communities. In 1942 the survivors were transferred to the new extermination camp at Auschwitz where they perished as part of the 'Final Solution'. In October 1939 over 1000 Jews from Moravská Ostrava were transferred to a an 'agricultural settlement' at Nisko, east of Lublin in occupied Poland. The camp was not ready and many died in the primitive autumn conditions. Others were driven by their SS guards across the Nazi-Soviet demarcation line into the Russian zone. Around 400 survivors returned to the Protectorate in the spring of 1940. The Nisko affair seems to have been part of an abortive Nazi plan to establish a 'Jewish reservation' in Poland. Before the deportations began, Jakub Edelstein, the deputy leader of the Prague Religious Community, was told by Eichmann that the aim was to transfer all the Jews in the Protectorate to the area. The Nisko experience left Edelstein convinced that almost anything was better than forced transfers to Poland.

The war brought an avalanche of new decrees aimed against the Jews. A dawn-to-dusk curfew was imposed on all Jewish households and their radios were confiscated. At the beginning of 1940 Jews were forbidden to withdraw more than 1,500 crowns a week from their bank accounts which were not allowed to earn interest. Gold, silver, platinum and jewellry were to be sold at a discount to Hadega, a special company dealing in Jewish property established at 32 Hibernergasse. Jews were excluded from the movie and theatre industries. They were restricted to the back of the second car on Prague trams and excluded from all hotels except the Fišer and the Star. In April 1940 the Protectorate government issued a comprehensive law banning Jews from public service and all social, cultural and economic organizations. Jewish doctors could still practice but only in the Jewish community

A still from the anti-Semitic propaganda film Jud Süss *(Jew Süss) part of which was shot at the Prague's Barrandov film studio*

and their numbers were severely restricted. Jews were ordered to report to the local police and have their identity papers stamped with a distinctive J. Further measures followed. In August 1940 Jewish children were excluded from Czech schools. The same month special shopping hours were imposed which ensured that others had the best chance of buying scarce items. In October 1940, special regulations issued by the Protectorate government denied Jews access to a wide range of rationed goods. Jews were banned from certain areas of Prague including the Vltava embankment. In January 1941 their driving licences were confiscated. Jews were forced out of apartments in the best areas of Prague and moved into old tenements in the First, Second and Fifth districts of the city. Their flats were taken over by Nazi officials. The Jewish Religious Congregation was meant to look after the welfare of those reduced to penury by these measures and to supply work details for such menial tasks as clearing snow from the runways at Ruzyně airfield. In January 1941 over 7000 Prague Jews were engaged in some form of forced labour.

Discrimination against the Jewish community culminated with the decree of 1 September 1941 ordering all Jews to wear the Yellow Star of David. At the same time Jews were forbidden to leave their local area without the written permission of the police. Although the Jewish community did not know it, these moves were the preliminary to the Final Solution, the deportation of the European Jews to a series of SS death camps under construction in occupied Poland, of which the most notorious was to be the huge complex at Auschwitz-Birkenau. On 27 September 1941, SS Obergruppenführer

Reinhard Heydrich, the head of the Nazi security police, was named acting Reichsprotektor, replacing Neurath at the Hradčany (see Chapter Three). His arrival in Prague prefigured the extinction of the Jewish community. Since the invasion of the Soviet Union in June 1941, Heydrich's killing squads, the SS Einsatzgruppen, had been engaged in the massacre of Russian Jews caught behind the front. On 31 July 1941, while this campaign was being launched in the East, Heydrich was also made responsible for the preparations necessary 'to bring about a complete solution of the Jewish question in the German sphere of influence in Europe.' With the Nazis now involved in total war, anti-Semitism had developed into mass murder, designed to create a New Order based on the annihilation of the European Jews.

One of Heydrich's first acts in Prague was to close the remaining synagogues and all other Jewish centres of worship. On 10 October 1941, he held a special planning meeting attended by Eichmann and Karl Hermann Frank which decided to begin deportations from the Protectorate to Łódź, Minsk and Riga. The process was to be controlled by Eichmann's Zentralstelle. The concentration of all Czech Jews in a single ghetto at the fortress town of Terezín (Theresienstadt), forty miles north of Prague, was also discussed. Six days later the first train containing 1000 Jews left Prague for Łódź. Between 16 October and 3 November a total of five transports containing nearly 5,000 men, women and children were despatched to the Lodž ghetto. Conditions were appalling and many died within months. The remainder were either worked to death or later perished in the extermination camps of Chełmno and Majdanek. Only a few individuals survived the war. At a second meeting in the Reichsprotektor's office on 17 October 1941, a final decision was announced on the creation of a ghetto at Terezín. According to Heydrich, the Jews of Bohemia/Moravia were to be 'concentrated for evacuation ... in one transit camp. For this purpose Theresienstadt has been completely evacuated by all units of the army ... The Czechs have been advised to move somewhere else ... 50,000 to 60,000 Jews can easily be housed in Theresienstadt. From there the Jews will be taken to the East ... After the complete evacuation of the Jews, Theresienstadt will be settled by Germans in accordance with perfect planning and will become a centre of German life.' Heydrich stressed the need for secrecy. Under no circumstances was anything to leak out about the this ultimate objective. The Jews were to think that Terezín was a labour camp, not a transit point to the killing centres further East.

On 24 November 1941 an Aufbaukommando (Construction group) of young Jewish men was despatched from Prague to Terezín to prepare the new ghetto. From the SS point of view, the town was an ideal site. It was surrounded by a twelve-sided wall with only six

A direction sign points the way to an air-raid shelter for 'Non-Aryans'

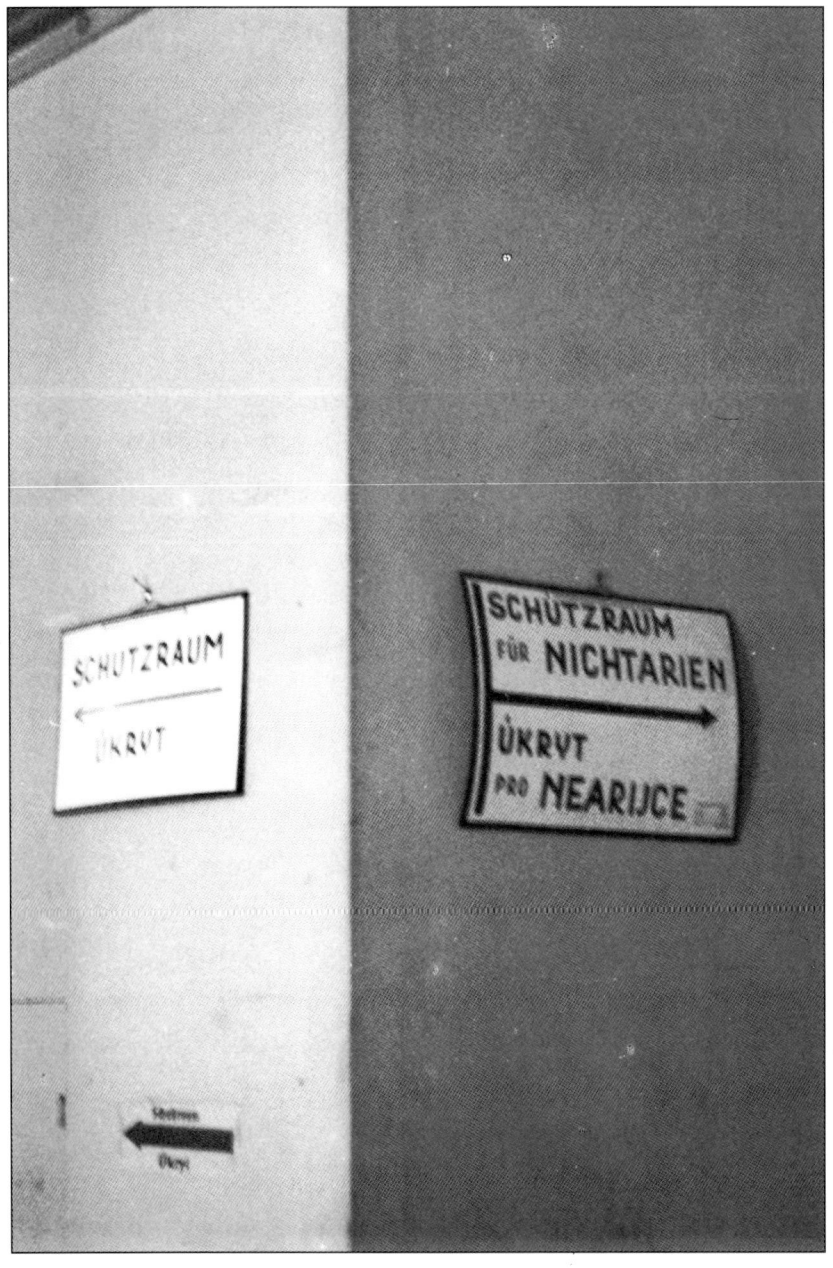

gates, making it easy to guard and isolate. It also contained large army barrack blocks which could be packed with deportees. Until the spring of 1942 the ghetto was confined to the military buildings in the town while the original Czech population remained in the regular housing. There was great pressure on space. Within days the first transports of men, women and children from Prague followed the original construction group which had been given no time to prepare proper living quarters. Men and women were packed into segregated buildings and there was great overcrowding. Each resident had less than two square meters of living space. The SS administration, under Hauptsturmführer Siegfried Seidl, an Austrian, was harsh and brutal. The inmates were confined to their barracks except for work details and death sentences were imposed for attempting to communicate with the remaining Czechs in the town or trading with them for black-market food and cigarettes.

The process of registering the persons and property of those deported to Terezín was assigned to the Jewish Religious Congregation of Prague under the supervision of Eichmann's representative, Hans Gunther.

A decree of 1 September 1941 required Jews to wear a yellow Star of David sewn on their clothes

In this way the Jews were made parties to their own destruction. The leadership, now headed by Jakub Edelstein and Otto Zucker, was in an almost impossible position. The Jewish community was isolated from any form of outside help. While some Czechs had at first supported the Jews as a form of opposition to the Nazis or from a sense of social solidarity, such gestures had become increasingly dangerous as German police controls tightened. By 1942 Czechs caught harbouring Jews had become liable to a death sentence, along with their entire family. In the SS terror which accompanied the arrival and later the assassination of Heydrich, few Czechs were prepared to take

Jewish women sorting property in a Prague synagogue

Religious objects were brought to Prague from all over the Protectorate

such risks. Only 484 Jews were able to survive the war as 'U-boats', submerging themselves in the Czech population. An uprising was not a feasible alternative. The Jews, like other Czech citizens, could only wage an armed struggle from abroad as part of the exile armies formed in Britain and the Soviet Union which contained a high proportion of Czech Jews. Passive resistance was also dangerous. Refusal to cooperate in the registration process threatened the survival of the whole community. When delays occurred in the registration of the first thousand Jews for deportation, Gunther's deputy, Obersturmbannführer Karl Rahm, accused the head of the Jewish emigration section and his deputy of sabotage. They were sent to Mauthausen as a warning to the rest of the Jewish community and died within twelve days. Edelstein and his colleagues had thus little alternative but to play for time in the hope that an allied victory would eventually save their community.

Before each deportation to Terezín, the families involved were notified by the Jewish

Jewish property was collected by the Nazis. Some objects were used to create a 'Central Jewish Museum' in Prague. The remainder was distributed to the SS and other Nazi organizations

leadership and assembled in a wired area with a few shabby huts established at the Trade Fair Grounds near Stromovka Park. Only a limited amount of luggage was allowed. Heda Margolius Kovaly, deported in the autumn of 1941, recalled the chaotic scene at the assembly centre: 'The inside of the Exposition Hall was like a medieval madhouse... Several people who were seriously ill and had been brought there on stretchers died on the spot. A Mrs Tausig went completely crazy, tore her false teeth out of her mouth, and threw them at our lord and master, Obersturmbannführer Fiedler. There were babies and small children who cried incessantly and, just beside my parents, a small fat bald man sat on his suitcase playing his violin as if none of the surrounding bedlam were any concern of his. He played Beethoven's Concerto in D Major, practising the same passages over and over again.'

From this assembly point the columns were marched through the streets, escorted by Czech police, to Prague-Bubny Station and the slow three-hour train journey to Terezín. The Jewish Congregation arranged for groups of volunteers to assist those too old or sick to carry their own cases. The deportations usually took place in the early hours of the morning to avoid any show of Czech sympathy with the victims. Such silent demonstrations, however, sometimes occurred. Margit Galat, who was part of a group which was marched to Bubny by daylight, later recalled the reaction of the Czech passersby, 'the men ostentatiously taking off their hats, many of the women weeping'. At the station the Jews were loaded into trains guarded by German police, with one officer and twelve men to each transport. At first passenger coaches were provided but these were soon replaced by freight cars which were packed to the doors without regard for age or sex. As Heda Margolius Kovaly recalled : 'Even though in the following years I would experience infinitely more gruelling transports, this one seemed to be the worst because it was first. If every beginning is hard, the beginning of hardship is the hardest.' Between 24 November 1941 and 16 March 1945, 122 trains were sent from all over the Protectorate to Terezín carrying 73,608 people. The last to go were Jewish partners in mixed marriages who were deported at the end of 1944. Their spouses were sent to a special labour camp at Bystřice near Benešov. As the deportations accelerated, Eichmann's Zentralstelle für jüdische Auswanderung changed its name to Zentralamt für die Regelung der Judenfrage in Böhmen und Mähren (Central Office for the Settlement of the Jewish Problem in Bohemia and Moravia), a title which fitted its true role in the Final Solution.

The property left behind in Prague was redistributed to Germans. The process was controlled by the SS which was besieged by demands for Jewish apartments and other forms of loot from the horde of bureaucrats who had descended on the city during the war. In an irate memorandum to Nazi officials in Prague, Stahlecker's successor as head of the security police, SS Standartenführer (Colonel) Horst Böhme, complained that his office was being treated as a housing agency. By 1944 9,288 apartments, formerly inhabited by 45,000 Jews, had been reassigned, often to SS officials and others with political influence. Forty-five warehouses in the city were stacked with confiscated goods. The Gestapo had first pick of furniture, typewriters, binoculars, cameras, adding machines and film projectors, all of which were supposedly needed by new police offices in the occupied areas. Other material went to Alfred Rosenberg's Ministry for the East or to the Nazi welfare organization, Winterhilfe, for distribution to refugees from the bombed cities of the Ruhr. It was an invitation to corruption on a massive scale and

Former Ceremonial Hall by the Old Jewish Cemetery

there was much bureaucratic squabbling over the loot. In this struggle, as in others, the SS had emerged on top by 1944.

The Nazis destroyed synagogues and Jewish graveyards in the Sudetenland. The synagogues of Prague and the ancient Jewish cemetery in the Old Town, however, were spared this fate. On 17 June 1942 the Protectorate government ordered the transfer of the archives and religious objects of all Jewish congregations to the capital where they accumulated in a former Jewish school at 3 Joachymgasse in the Old Town. The provincial department of the Jewish Congregation of Prague under Dr Karel Stein was made responsible for registering and cataloguing this collection which included 2,500 Torah rolls, 6000 pieces of ceremonial silver and a huge archive of papers and photographs relating to Jewish life. Stein suggested that this material should be used as the basis for a Central Jewish Museum, augmenting the holdings of the Jewish Museum of Prague founded in 1906 when urban renewal destroyed the old ghetto. His idea was to save these unique items in the hope that they could be restored to their proper owners after the war. Gunther's deputy at the Zentralstelle, SS Obersturmbannführer (Lieutenant Colonel) Karl Rahm, agreed to this project. For the SS, the collection was to form the basis of a museum of the extinct Jewish race after the Final Solution had been

Torah rolls (Jewish holy scriptures) confiscated and catalogued by the Nazis when they closed Czech synagogues

The Spanish Synagogue in the old Jewish quarter of Prague

The Jewish community was forced to register for deportation to the new ghetto established by the Nazis at Terezín

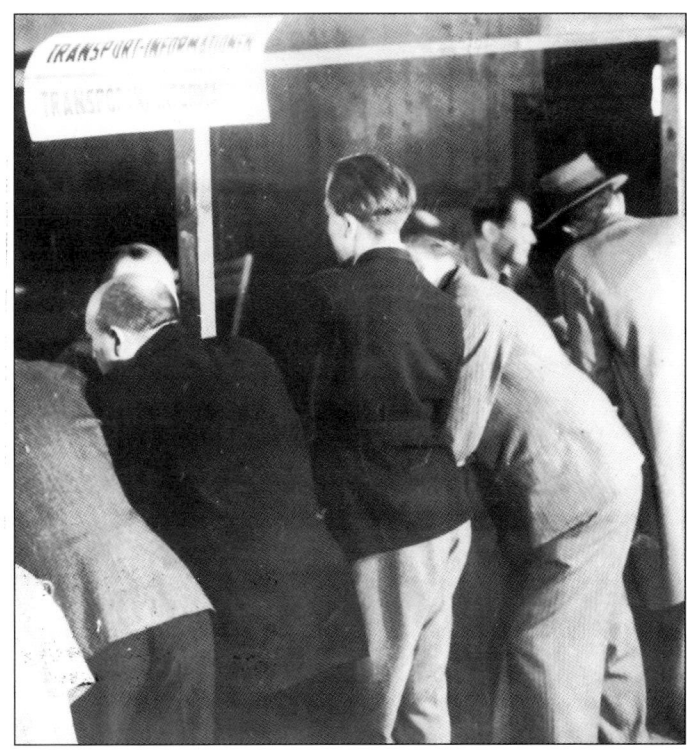

concluded. Prague was perhaps chosen for this macabre project because it was here that the Jewish leaders had supposedly conspired to take over the world, a myth perpetrated by the spurious 'Protocols of the Elders of Zion', a clumsy nineteenth-century forgery by the Russian secret police which had passed into Nazi ideology. The synagogues of the Old Town were selected to display the collections which were catalogued by a small Jewish staff. Years later, when an American Jewish scholar examined a selection of the Torah rolls, a small note fell from one. It read: 'Please God, help us in these troubled times.' As part of the museum project, restoration work began on the synagogue

buildings. In November 1942, the SS gave permission for an exhibition of Jewish books and manuscripts in the High Synagogue. The following year there was a second exhibition on 'Jewish Life from the Cradle to the Grave' in the Klausen Synagogue. It was toured by high-ranking SS officers who suggested only small changes in the displays. For these men, already deeply implicated in the Final Solution, the title of the exhibition had a grisly significance for they knew that the grave was the immediate fate awaiting the entire Jewish community. By this stage the first deportations of the Jewish museum staff had already begun and by 1944 they had all been sent to Terezín. Most were to perish in the SS death camps further East.

The leadership of the Jewish Congregation of Prague went to Terezín with the rest of the community and became responsible for administering the ghetto. It was soon clear that the SS had lied and that the fortress was not the final destination of the Czech Jews. As early as January 1942 the first transport was sent from Terezín to Riga. The SS dictated the numbers in each transport but it was up to the Jewish leadership to select the individuals involved. Some were exempted because they were essential to the running of the camp or because they belonged to political groups like the Communists and the Zionists who drew up their own exemption lists. But in the end the leaders faced an agonizing choice. They either obeyed the SS and singled out individuals for deportation or they risked indiscriminate action by the Nazis against the entire community. The leaders chose to save some by sacrificing others. Knowing nothing of the real nature of the Final Solution, they believed that the deported Jews were being taken to labour camps further East where conditions might be bad, but where there was still some hope of survival.

In 1942 Heydrich gave Terezín another function, as an 'old people's ghetto' for the German Jews. As with its designation as a labour camp for Czech Jews, this was a cynical manoeuvre designed to camouflage the real nature of the Final Solution. In 1942 transports poured in carrying German Jews over 65 and other categories exempt from direct deportation to the East. Between July and September 1942 over 40,000 arrived, the majority over 70. Many quickly died from lack of medical care and poor food. Others were shipped to the East once the legend of the 'old people's ghetto' had served its purpose, sharing the fate of the Czech Jews deported to make room for them

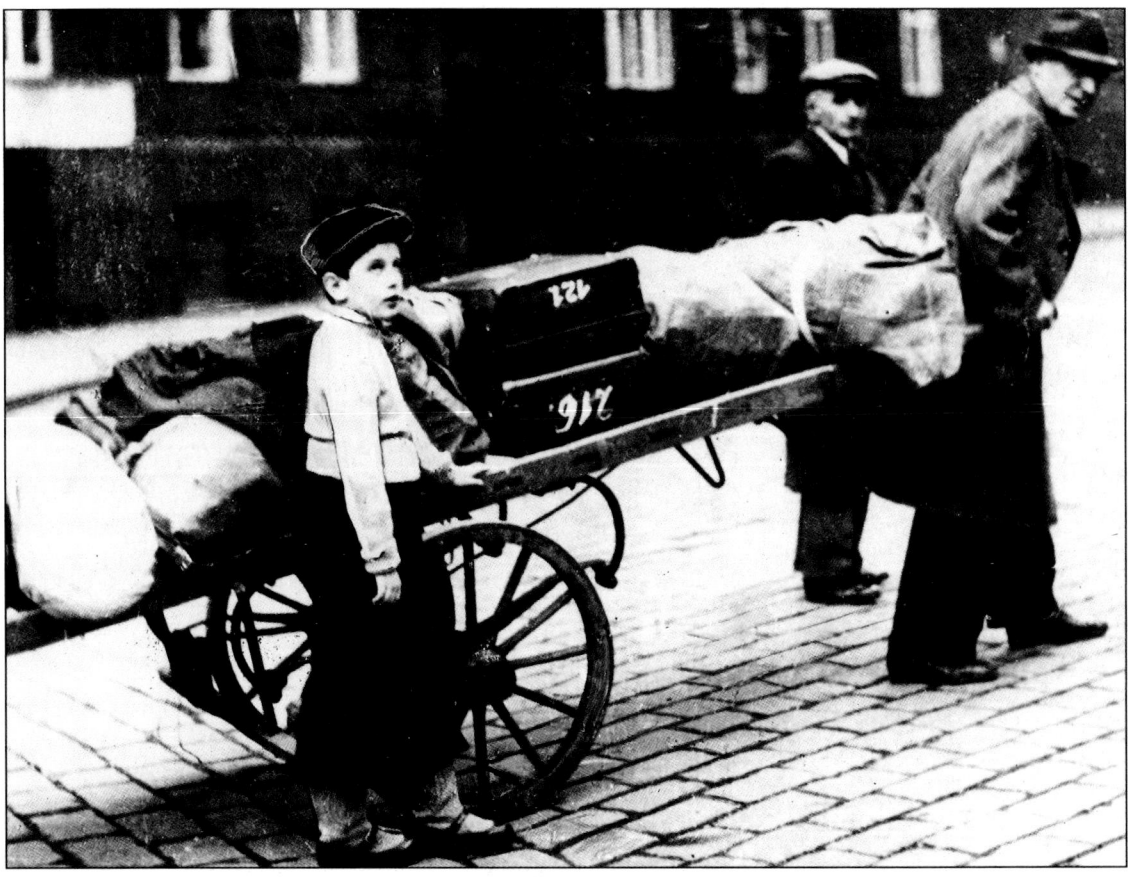

Deportees were allowed to take only a limited amount of property to Terezín

Prague-Bubny railway station

in Terezín. By the summer of 1942 the ghetto had expanded to fill the whole town. The SS rarely entered the gates and the inhabitants were allowed a measure of autonomy. Terezín had its own special currency, shops, a theatre, even an orchestra and a jazz band. But people lived from day to day, never knowing when the call would come to assemble for the journey to the East. At first most of the transports went to the Łódź ghetto, but from October 1942 they went straight to the vast death factory at Auschwitz-Birkenau. Between then and the last transport in October 1944, 25 trains were despatched from Terezín to Auschwitz carrying 44,839 men, women and children. Of these

Jewish deportees arriving at Terezín

Samples of banknotes specially designed for use inside the ghetto at Terezín

80 per cent were immediately gassed and 90 per cent did not survive the war. One group was killed without even passing through Terezín. On 9 June 1942, 1000 Prague Jews were despatched directly to Poland as a reprisal for the assassination of Heydrich (see Chapter Three). Their transport bore the designation AaH (Attentat auf Heydrich/Assassination of Heydrich). Only one man survived by jumping from a train. They were followed by a further 2000 from Terezín who met their deaths at 'an unknown destination in the East'.

The Nazis continued to camouflage the Final Solution from its victims. In September 1943 two trains containing over 5000 men, women and children were sent to Auschwitz-Birkenau. They were not killed immediately but isolated in a special 'family camp'. In December 1943 another 5000 followed. Three months later the prisoners were told by the SS that they were being transferred to a new labour camp and given postcards to send to relatives in Terezín. Many suspected what was about to happen for it was impossible totally to conceal what was going on at Auschwitz. They used the opportunity to convey warnings to those left behind in the Protectorate. After staging this sham, the SS sent the occupants of the 'family camp' to the gas chambers. It was said that they went to their deaths singing the Czechoslovak national anthem. Despite the coded postcard warnings which escaped SS censorship, many in Terezín still refused to believe what was happening in the East. Siegfried Lederer, a prisoner in the 'family camp', escaped and returned to Terezín where he warned the Jewish leader, Rabbi Leo Baeck, about the SS campaign of genocide. Baeck, however, was reluctant to inform the people, feeling that he was powerless to end the killing and wishing to spare them knowledge of their ultimate fate.

While the SS tried to delude the inhabitants of Terezín, it was still using Terezín to fool the world. In October 1943, 300 Danish Jews arrived in the ghetto. The remainder, warned in advance about the Nazi round-up, had escaped to Sweden. There was uproar in Copenhagen and the neutral Swedes, whom the Nazis were anxious to placate for economic reasons, began to ask awkward questions. The Danish Jews were therefore treated as a privileged group and the SS agreed to a Red Cross inspection of Terezín. In April 1944 the new commandant, Obersturmbannführer Karl Rahm, ordered a 'beautification' campaign. Flowerbeds were laid out and the buildings were painted. Staged events were planned to impress the delegation. One of the prisoners, Mordechai Ansbacher, then a fourteen-year-old boy, later recalled: 'We would get our instructions that it was time to put on a show ... when it was time for an international inspection party, the children were rehearsed in a football game and there was ice cream – which we were not allowed to eat'. At the same time another 7,500 people were deported to the East to reduce overcrowding. Amongst those who perished was the former leader of the Prague Jewish Congregation, Jakub Edelstein. Arrested by the previous commandant of Terezín, Anton Burger, an Austrian with a special hatred for Czech Jews, he had been held in the prison cells at Auschwitz since November 1943. In June 1944, Edelstein was reunited with his family for the last time. Before Mrs Edelstein was deported from Terezín she was told by Eichmann that she was going to meet her husband. As one witness recalled: 'Yes. She saw him ... She saw him at the door of Crematorium No. 3. All of them were gassed.'

The Red Cross inspection took place on 23 June 1944. The team, two Danes and a Swiss, seemed impressed by the Nazi experiment in 'Jewish self-government.' As Ansbacher remarked: 'The Nazis feared the International Red Cross, or what they would say to the Americans if they found out the truth. They so beautified the concentration camp that the Red Cross accepted it as a sort of resort. They never saw the horrible conditions that really existed there.' The inspection committee 'saw only the new, healthy inmates, who were the only ones allowed on the streets.' Eichmann was so pleased with the results that he planned a documentary film on the ghetto for international release, but this project was never completed. The transformation of Terezín into a 'model ghetto' meant no respite for the inhabitants of the camp, apart from those in privileged categories. In September/October 1944 more than 18,000 people were deported to the East where the weak were gassed and the strong used as forced labour. Seventy per cent of those left in Terezín were women and the majority of the men were over 65. Despite the accelerating collapse of Nazi power, the last transport left Prague for Terezín as late as 16 March 1945, containing the Jewish members of mixed marriages who had previously enjoyed a protected status.

Bilingual road signs at the junction near Prague's Bubny railway station seen in the left background. It was from here that the Prague Jews were deported

In the spring of 1945 Terezín was again used as a show ghetto as part of the desperate attempt by the head of the SS, Heinrich Himmler, to negotiate a compromise peace with the Americans in the final months of the war. In an attempt to deny the Holocaust, the SS destroyed all camp records for the period before 1945 and agreed to another visit by the International Red Cross. On 6 April the Swiss representative, Paul Dunant, arrived at Terezín and was shown around the camp by Eichmann in person. Despite the best efforts of the SS, he was not deceived. In a report to Geneva, Dunant remarked: 'More interesting that the actual living conditions... was the question whether it had indeed merely served as a transit camp and how many deportations to the East had taken place.' On his last visit to Terezín, four days later, Eichmann was unrepentant about his own role in the Final Solution, remarking that when the time came he would 'gladly jump into the pit, knowing that in the same pit there are five million enemies of the state'.

By this stage the survivors of the ghetto knew the terrible reality of the Holocaust. They had learned the truth from transports of concentration camp prisoners evacuated from the East in the face of the advancing Red Army. These newcomers were infested with lice and in April 1945 a typhus epidemic broke out which had soon claimed hundreds victims. Shortly afterwards the SS tried to assemble two transports for an unknown destination. Fearing that the Nazis intended to cover up their crimes by staging a massacre in the last days of the war, the ghetto leaders refused to cooperate and smuggled a warning to the Red Cross in Prague. On 19 April 1945, Dunant approached Frank and obtained his promise that there would be no more deportations from Terezín. Anxious to open negotiations with the Americans, Frank was now posing as a moderate, using the surviving Jews as evidence of his goodwill (see Chapter Four). On 2 May 1945 the SS guards fled from Terezín and two days later a group of Czech volunteers arrived to help the ghetto medical staff fight the typhus epidemic which had already claimed the lives of 44 doctors and nurses. On 8 May the first units of the Red Army appeared and placed Terezín under strict quarantine. By June the outbreak was over and the prisoners were able to leave. But liberation had come too late for most of the Czech Jews. Of 39,395 deported to Terezín from Prague, 31,709 had perished, either in the ghetto or in the death camps further East. Of the 92,199 Jews who had lived in Bohemia/Moravia in 1941, only 14,045 had survived the war.

Judgement was soon delivered on those who had implemented the Final Solution in the Czech lands. Heydrich was already dead, assassinated by Czech parachute agents from Britain in May 1942. His successor Daluege and the real power behind the throne in Prague, Karl Hermann Frank, were hanged by the Czechs in 1946. Eichmann's representative in the Protectorate, Hans Gunther, was killed by partisans on 5 May 1945 as he tried to flee to Germany. Of the three wartime commandants of Terezín, Seidl and Rahm were extradited from the American zone of Austria and executed at Litoměřice in April 1947. Burger, who faced the same fate, escaped from a US internment camp before he could be handed over. On 11 April 1945 Adolf Eichmann disappeared from Terezín and a month later, disguised as a Luftwaffe corporal, surrendered to American troops in Bavaria. In the confusion of the Nazi collapse he remained unrecognized and was able to live under cover. Five years later he fled to Latin America. But he was tracked to Buenos Aires by Israeli agents in May 1960 and kidnapped to face justice. After a public trial in Jerusalem, Eichmann went to the gallows on 31 May 1962 without a word of remorse. Summing up the case against the accused, the Israeli prosecutor, Gideon Hausner, remarked: 'In this courtroom, the shades of Hitler and his accomplices are around us. They are ghouls which humanity will never forget.'

'If the Gestapo caught us, it meant death not only for us but for anyone who helped us or was even casually associated with us . . . [The people of Prague] all had their own lives and their own wartime concerns. Nothing, perhaps, as horrible as what we had been through, but all suffering can become intolerable. Maybe some of them were as worn out by running into shelters and standing in lines for food as we were by the terrors of the camps'

HEDA MARGOLIUS KOVALY : *PRAGUE FAREWELL*

CHAPTER SIX

Occupational Hazards

A map of 'Hitler's New Europe' on display in a Prague shop window

The German Minister of Propaganda Joseph Goebbels during his visit to Prague with the Charles Bridge in the background

IN OCTOBER 1939 a blackout was imposed on Prague which darkened the streets, dimmed the lights of cars and trams and shuttered apartment windows. Even pocket torches were restricted to a narrow beam. It was a serious offence to show a light which could become an aiming point for enemy bombers. Street corners, curbs and projecting walls were painted with a white stripe to prevent unwary pedestrians from injuring themselves in the dark. An Air Raid Precautions Service was created and the Fire Brigade prepared to deal with incendiary attacks. The bombers did not come until November 1944 but claimed an early victim in October 1939 when Republika, an open-air cinema in Prague-Žižkov with Man' who was rumoured to leap from murky alleyways into the paths of passersby. In fact there was little street crime during the occupation, not least because of random police checks and the possibility of detention by the Gestapo.

Along with the blackout came rationing. At first the Czech standard of living held up under the strain of war and some social groups found themselves better off than before. Allowances of flour and sugar were more generous in Bohemia/Moravia than in the Reich while the meat allocation was the same. Only the fat ration was lower. A wide range of consumer goods from pre-war stocks remained on sale long after they had vanished

A group of German officers sightseeing in Old Town Square

a capacity of 700, was closed down by the air-raid regulations. The blackout imposed a new way of life on the Czechs. In the winter evenings the streets were deserted after the last cinema performance and people stayed indoors. In the last years of the war, coal and gas shortages left apartments unheated and provided further encouragement to go to bed early. The result was a soaring wartime birthrate as Czechs turned to sex as the only game in town. The blackout generated its own urban legends. One was the 'Razor Blade Man', a slasher who was supposed to hunt women through the darkened streets of the city. Another was the 'Spring from the shelves of German shops. The film actress, Adina Mandlová, who spent some months in Berlin in 1942, was shocked by the shortage of food, drink and cigarettes in the capital of the Reich. She was kept going by parcels of delicacies from an admirer in Prague with black-market connexions. When she returned home and complained about the food situation in Germany, she was warned about spreading rumours harmful to the Reich, an offence that carried the death sentence. But for the Germans, Prague, like Paris, was a desirable posting. Impressed by the absence of allied bombing and the easy availability of scarce consumer goods, they

called the Protectorate 'the land of smiles'. As the war intensified, efforts were made to increase food production. Throughout the city, parks and open spaces were ploughed up to grow potatoes and other vegetables. Many inhabitants of Prague began to breed rabbits for the pot, fattening them on grass collected in the diminishing amount of leisure time left by the voracious demands of the armaments factories. They could also supplement their basic allowances on the black-market, or by 'under the counter' purchases of scarce items from their regular shopkeepers. This was a dangerous business, however, for the Gestapo treated rationing offences as sabotage and there were regular crackdowns on illegal trading.

The Nazis cultivated the working class whose contribution was vital for the efficient operation of war industry. German orders soaked up unemployment and offered the chance of higher wages. The Nazis boasted that between March 1939 and December 1940, average wages had increased by 40–45 per cent. Working-class income was also boosted by the increasing mobilization of women. Under Heydrich, who posed as a friend of the workers, extra supplies of tobacco and shoes were distributed to the arms factories. Heavy workers were given a new fat ration on the same scale as in the Reich. As Heydrich remarked in his secret speech of 2 October 1941, the Czechs must have their swill. In a propaganda gesture, he received a delegation of the Czech Labour Front (NOÚZ) at the Hradčany and opened the hotels of fashionable resorts like Karlovy Vary for workers' holidays. This was all part of the myth that the Nazis were fighting both Bolshevism and plutocracy while offering the workers equality and social justice. By contrast those on fixed incomes, professionals, civil servants and teachers were worse off than before the war. The Czech middle class was further affected by the concentration of industry after 1941 which closed small and medium-sized enterprises and favoured the heavy industrial, chemical and electrical sectors. Those affected by this process were either redeployed to the armaments factories or conscripted for war work in Germany. From the Nazi point of view the aim of industrial concentration was not only to increase the volume of arms production but also to Germanize key economic sectors and undermine Czech businesses. The destruction of the Jews further weakened the social and economic basis of the Czech middle class, a fact that 'turned out to be of paramount importance for the country's political development in the late 1940s' since it paved the way for extensive nationalization.

As the war progressed, rationing intensified. Examples of food, soap and coal coupons

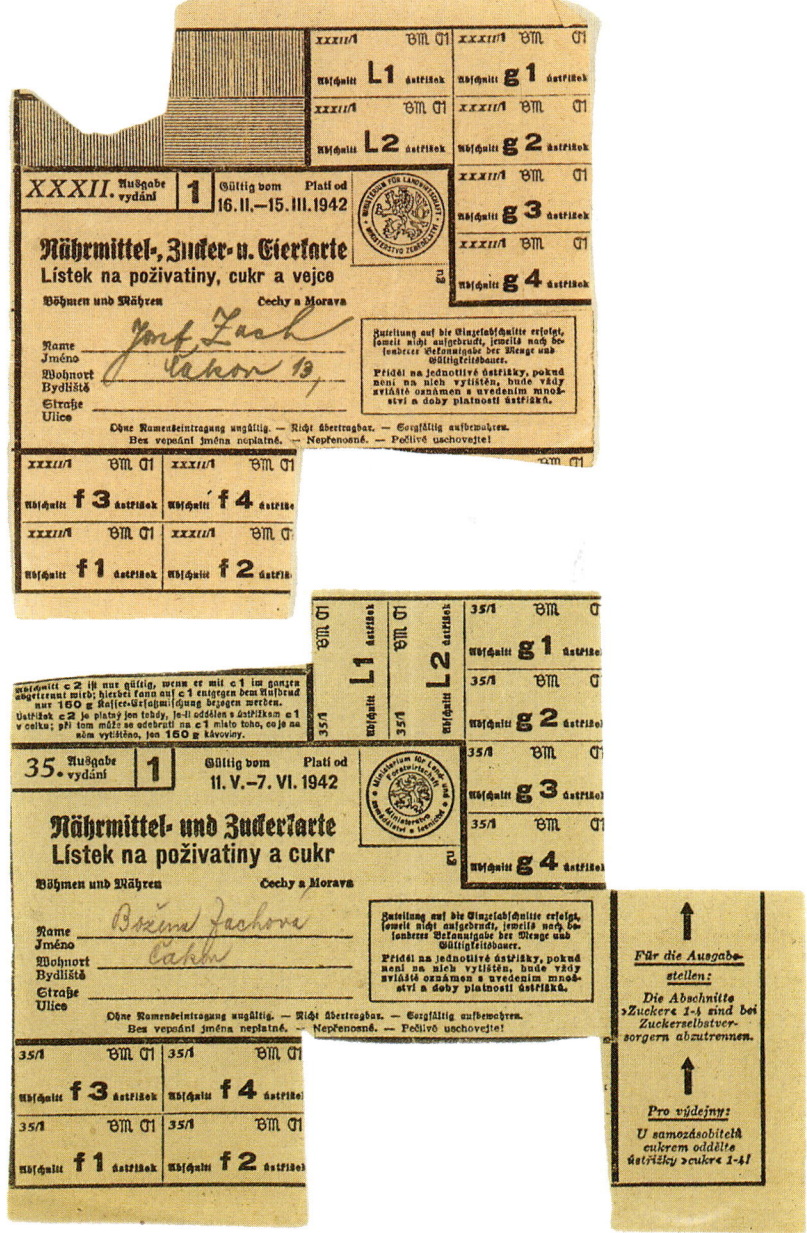

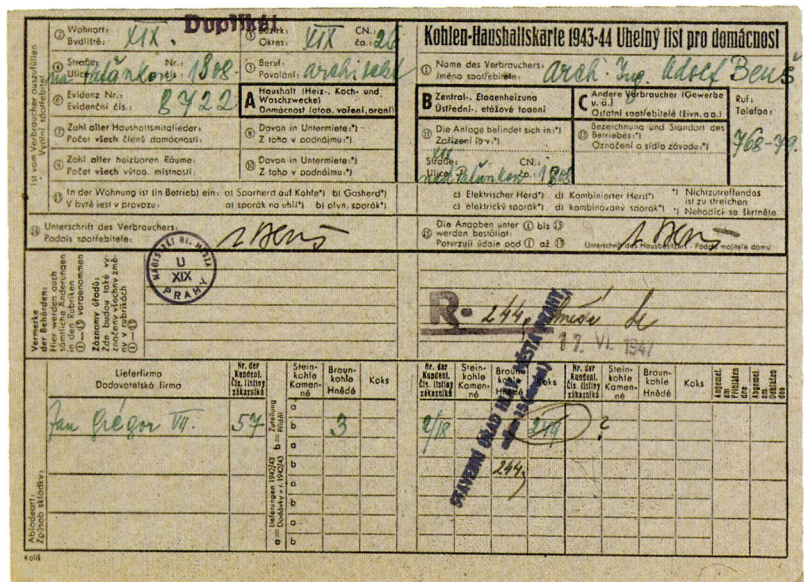

dramatically. By February 1943 all men aged between 16 and 65 and all women aged between 17 and 45 had become liable to industrial conscription. Many women chose to become pregnant during this period in order to avoid war work. Certain classes of children as young as 16 could also be called up for service in the Reich as well as in Bohemia/Moravia. The Germans argued that since the Czechs had not been asked to fight, they must contribute their labour to the defence of the Nazi New Order. At the same time benefits were eroded and wages were frozen. In the last two years of the Protectorate, rations were restricted. In the autumn of 1944, the average weekly allowance was one egg, a quarter kilo of meat (usually horse),

A restaurant on Strosmayer Square advertising in Czech and German

By the end of the war, conditions had worsened for everyone. In February 1945 the working week in the arms factories was officially extended to 64 hours. In practice working hours expanded even further with twelve-hour shifts and six-day weeks. Ten-hour shifts on Sundays were also frequently demanded. In order to meet these demands, employees of plants on the outskirts of Prague had to leave home at 04:00 and did not return until 22:00. Workers had to carry a labour book and could not change jobs without the consent of their employer. Between 1941 and 1943 the ranks of those mobilized for compulsory labour expanded

one thousand and fifty-two grams of bread and three and a half kilos of potatoes. There was also a monthly allowance of one hundred and forty grams of butter, sixty grams of fat, one hundred and sixty grams of artificial fat, one thousand two hundred grams of sugar and sixteen bread rolls. The cigarette ration declined from thirty-five to twenty-five a week.

By 1944 coffee was only obtainable on the black market where it cost up to one thousand eight hundred crowns a kilo. Other black-market prices also soared. A cigarette cost twenty crowns, a single egg twenty-five

crowns and a bottle of spirits over eight hundred crowns. Restaurants resorted to desperate expedients. One luxury establishment continued to sell escargots by recycling empty snail shells filled with finely chopped offal. Shops ran out of stock, clearing even displays of scarce items which had been left in place for propaganda purposes. Many were closed and the staff redeployed to war industry. The empty windows displayed signs stating: 'Closed for the victory of the Reich.' The streets were piled with huge heaps of stinking garbage because the labour was unavailable to take it away. Posters urged consumers to save gas and electricity. Hospitals, public buildings and apartment blocks were left without heating in the middle of a cold winter. In February 1945, however, electricity consumption had to be reduced by 30 per cent because of coal shortages caused by disruption of the rail network. At the same time the ration period was stretched out from 8 to 9 weeks and the Protectorate government had to appeal to the population for donations of shoes and warm clothing for Czech workers.

The transport system deteriorated under wartime conditions. By the middle of the war only privileged groups like doctors were still allowed private cars. Petrol shorages meant that buses and lorries were powered by coal gas, carried in a sausage-shaped balloon on the roof. At the end of 1944 all private cars were banned and remaining stocks of tyres

A 'Soap by ration ticket only' sign

An envelope specially printed for Hitler's birthday on 20 April 1942

A crowded Prague tram with the station stops in Czech and German

A Prague tram ticket

were requisitioned by the Germans. The Czech comedian, Vlasta Burian, resolved this problem by driving around the city in a coach pulled by five matched horses. Others relied on bicycles which became important possessions during the Protectorate. The increased demand sent prices soaring and by 1944 even a second-hand bike could cost up to one thousand five hundred crowns. Most ordinary Czechs had to rely on the extensive tram system that linked most points in the city. Wartime trams were dirty, crowded and increasingly dangerous

because of poor maintenance and lack of spares. There were three serious accidents in the last eighteen months of the war, caused by brake failures on steep hills. The authorities, however, blamed the passengers, claiming that the trams had been overloaded. In late 1944, journeys by train outside the city became dangerous because of low-flying American fighters which roved the railway lines looking for something to attack. A pilot diving on his target at high speed was in no position to discriminate between a German troop train and an ordinary express full of civilians.

The occupation increased the role of the state in every aspect of Czech life. In order to obtain new identity documents as citizens of the Protectorate, Czechs had to sign a declaration that they were not gypsies or Jews and prove it by providing a family tree covering both sets of grandparents. People

All car registration plates bore the stamp of the Protectorate

An advertisement for the technically advanced Czech Tatra car, popular with SS officers

Even parking tickets, like this one for a fine of 10 crowns, were bilingual

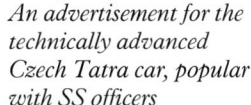

The corner of Hybernská Street during the Occupation

◀ *The cover of a handbook on the use of gas fuels*

K. H. Frank's armoured Mercedes Benz 540 K

had also to register for ration cards and labour service. After Heydrich's assassination all households had to register every occupant over the age of fifteen with the police. Travellers had to report to the police within twenty-four hours of their arrival at a new destination. It was a capital offence to shelter an unregistered person or to fail to register yourself. It was also dangerous to be caught without the proper papers by random security checks in the streets or on public transport. During the worst periods of the SS terror, people became neurotic about their identity cards, for to be found without one meant detention by the Gestapo and often death. Heda Margolius Kovaly, who escaped from a concentration-camp transport and reached Prague early in 1945, recalled the

A sign urging the population to save electricity, gas and water

An advertisement for luxury cigarettes at the beginning of the war

strain of living as a 'submarine' or 'illegal' without papers: 'Air raids were as dangerous as street cars. The police and air-raid wardens checked the papers of all strangers who entered the shelters but if you tried to stay in the street, which was strictly forbidden, you would almost surely be seen.' She was reluctant to seek shelter with the few friends who offered to hide her for fear of the consequences for their children if she was caught. It was another example of the Nazis forcing their victims to police themselves. With rationing and registration came queues for everything from procuring new identity cards to buying scarce items like tobacco. The saddest queues of all were the long columns of Jews, standing in line to register for deportation to Terezín and the gas chambers of Auschwitz-Birkenau.

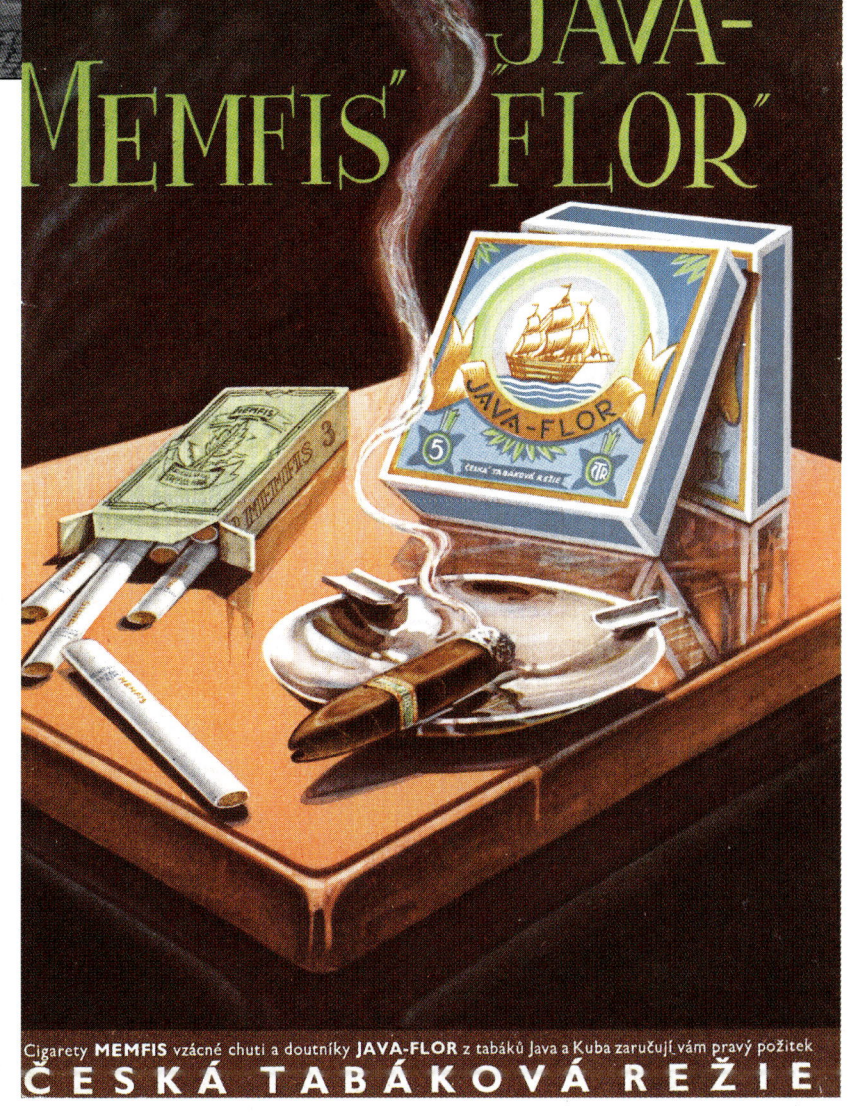

The new currency, in two languages, imposed by the Germans

Newly-weds posing against a background of SS signs

Specially decorated trams were hired for weddings

Public health deteriorated under the psychological and physical demands of the war. Professor Vladimír Vondráček, an eminent Prague psychiatrist, noted the effects of long hours, poor rations and the constant threat posed by the Gestapo and its informers. Infectious diseases like tuberculosis, dysentery, and hepatitis became common because of the bad diet which weakened natural resistance. There were also outbreaks of typhoid. The permanent state of tension maintained by the Germans, which deliberately destroyed normal social life and isolated individuals from each other, encouraged stress-related illnesses such as heart attacks, stomach ulcers and skin diseases, while many women reported irregular periods. The total mobilization of labour in 1944 produced many cases of nervous exhaustion and other kinds of mental disturbance as people were faced with long hours and the threat that their families would be broken up to work in different parts of the Protectorate or the Reich. There was a general sense of insecurity and fear even amongst children. The bombing that marked the final months of the war merely increased these strains and the effects of the occupation on Czech health were evident long after 1945.

Until the autumn of 1944, a series of leisure activities offered some relief from the pressures of war and occupation. When the Germans marched into Prague, they immediately assumed control of cultural policy. A special cultural section was established in the Reichsprotektor's office under the former German press attaché, Karl von Gregory, who served until 1941 when Heydrich replaced him with an SS officer named Martin Wolff. Newspapers were censored and became little more than propaganda sheets. Popular magazines, like *Zpravodaj* (Correspondent), confined war news to a single page and offered their readers a mixture of romantic stories, nature studies and features on exotic places like Indonesia and Japan. This format was so bland that one issue was much like another. Censorship extended not only to newspapers but also to books, music and drama. The works of the famous Czech historian, Palacký, were banned because they did not reflect the 'Wenceslas tradition' and the spirit of the New Europe. As part of their war on the intellectuals, the Nazis encouraged writing which celebrated the working class and provided an eerie taste of what was to come after the war. In March 1942, they sponsored a competition for

A street scene outside Prague's main station

A Nazi art exhibition at the Myslbek Gallery in Na Příkopě Street

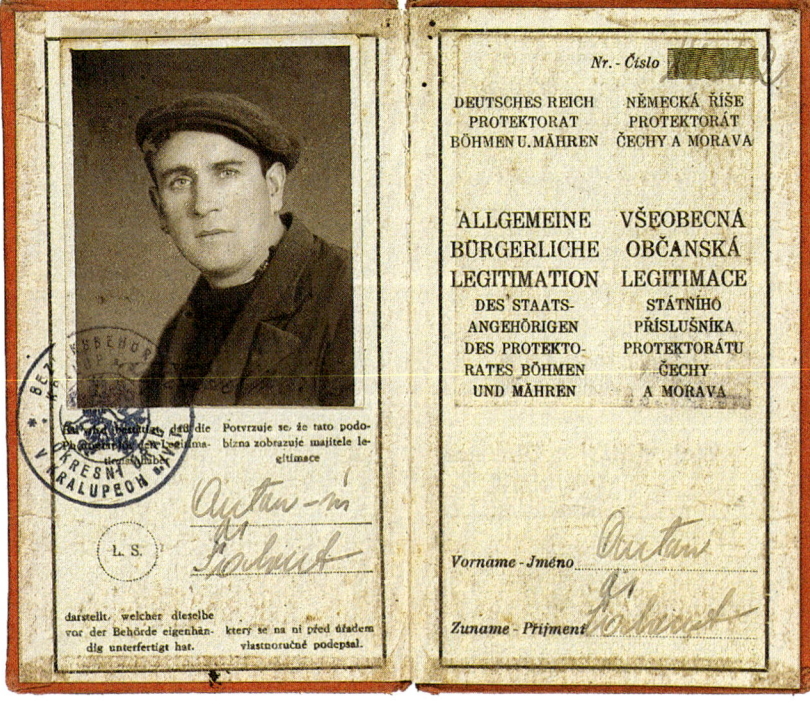

An identity card issued to citizens of the Protectorate

novels, poetry and short stories on the life of the workers. The winners included pieces entitled *The Boys in Blue Overalls, Men under Prague* and *Woven from Smoke* which were supposed to celebrate 'the union of the spirit and the hands' in Czech factories. In the musical field, patriotic pieces by Smetana and Dvořák were dropped and orchestras had to find less well-known works by Czech composers. The Czech National Theatre remained in business and was visited by several leading Nazis. Goebbels was impressed by the performance of Smetana's *Bartered Bride* which he attended there in November 1940. Survival was not without its price, however, and after the liberation the director, Václav Talich, was accused of collaboration. It was many years before he was rehabilitated.

In the long term the Nazis planned to Germanize culture. A start was made by restrictions on Czech composers and the promotion of German classics. As part of this process the Berlin Philharmonic Orchestra under Wilhelm Furtwängler visited Prague in November 1940 for a concert that included Beethoven's Seventh Symphony, the *Eulenspiegel* and *the Moldau*. In October 1941, Frank proclaimed Prague a city of German art and music, Mozart's 'second home'. Heydrich attended a gala performance of *Don Giovanni* at the Standtheater, where the opera was first staged, and a special stamp was issued to celebrate the occasion. The Palacký Bridge was renamed in honour of the composer as was Smetana Square in front of the Rudolfinum. Heydrich built up a German Philharmonic Opera in Prague and restored the Rudolfinum, since 1919 the seat of the Czechoslovak parliament, as a German concert hall. Just before his assassination on 27 May 1942, he also inaugurated Prague Music Week which opened with a performance of the works of his father, the failed composer Bruno

Heydrich, in the Wallenstein Palace. After Heydrich's death, the annual Prague Music Week was dedicated to his memory by Karl Hermann Frank.

The theatre was popular with both Czechs and Germans. The Nazis took over several theatres in Prague, such as the Stavovské Divadlo, for their own productions, but refrained at first from a direct attack on the Czech stage. In the opening years of the war there were a number of new productions, both professional and amateur. For many Czechs, drama groups provided the kind of social contact that could no longer be found in other forms of organization banned because of their association with nationalism, such as the sports association, SOKOL. A broad selection of plays was staged in Prague, ranging from Shakespeare and Sophocles to new pieces by young Czech writers. Popular film actresses like Adina Mandlová appeared in stage productions both in Prague and in the provinces. The Germans gradually clamped down on serious theatre, however, particularly after the assassination of Heydrich when all forms of Czech self-expression were severely restricted. A meeting at the National Theatre in June 1942 adopted the line advocated by the Czech propaganda minister, Emmanuel Moravec, resolving that Czech drama 'must help pacify the spirit of Bohemia and Moravia by an enhanced co-operation with Germany' and demanding the removal of the 'old trees' of nationalism from the cultural garden. As the war intensified, the theatres increasingly turned to escapism, not only to avoid political controversy but also to provide what audiences wanted. An advertisement in *Böhmen und Mähren* for February 1943 revealed a Prague stage dominated by Strauss operas and romantic comedies. In November 1944 the theatres were closed as part of the total mobilization and the actors were assigned to war industry.

If high culture was severely restricted by the Germans, they were less harsh on popular entertainment, the culture of the masses. Goebbels recognized that to work efficiently, people must be offered some escape from the pressures of the war. Speaking at a broadcasting exhibition in July 1939 he remarked : 'What is needed is not heavy, serious programmes which, after all, only a fraction of the people can grasp; we must provide the broad masses and millions of our people, engaged as they are in the struggle for existence, with as much relaxation and entertainment, edification and improvement, as possible.' For Czech radio audiences, 'edification and improvement' meant concerts, war news, and attacks on the exiles by Moravec. Special occasions like the arrival of Heydrich were covered live and in full by Czech commentators. Entertainment consisted of variety shows and light music. Sometimes comedy sketches had a political slant. The most notorious was *Stars over Baltimore*, an anti-Semitic satire broadcast on 6 December 1941, the day before the Japanese attack on Pearl Harbor, which portrayed Beneš as a tool of the Jews. One of the acts

The Standetheater, one of the main German cultural centres in Prague. This stamp commemorates the first performance of Mozart's Don Giovanni *there in October 1787*

K. H. Frank with Nazi cultural officials on a tour of inspection at Barrandov

A poster for a Dvořák concert at Prague's Lucerna in October 1944

Joseph Goebbels congratulating the Czech conductor Vaclav Talich after the performance of Smetana's Bartered Bride *at the National Theatre*

featured the famous comedian Vlasta Burian, the Czech Groucho Marx, in the role of an alcoholic Jan Masaryk, the foreign minister of the exile government. For this offence, Burian became one of the few Czech entertainers tried for collaboration after the war and his career never fully recovered.

Light music was on offer in the bars, dance halls and beer gardens of the city. The most popular singer of the period was R. A. Dvorský, a crooner in the Bing Crosby style, who had a series of wartime hits with songs like 'Bel-ami' and 'Chladné polibky', some of which were Czech cover versions of German records. Jazz was popular amongst many younger Czechs who had discovered swing before the occupation. The Nazis frowned on jazz as racially degenerate, the product of Blacks and Jews and a symbol of all that was wrong with America. The Gestapo cracked down on 'swing youth' both in the Reich and in the Protectorate. In a letter to Heydrich on 26 January 1942, Himmler ordered the destruction of the movement. The ringleaders were to be imprisoned at hard labour in concentration camps. Their parents were also to be detained and their property confiscated. According to Himmler, only by such brutal measures could this

MÓDA a jiné zájmy ženy

A fashion page from a Czech magazine

Módní klobouk - zdánlivě tak jednoduchý - je svou důmyslnou konstrukcí malý

A page from a film-fan magazine

threat to the stability of the home front be contained. Despite this draconian order, jazz continued to be played, both for its own sake and as a symbol of resistance to the Nazis. The records of Andy Kirk, Chick Webb and Jimmy Lunceford, which inspired youthful enthusiasts like the later novelist Josef Škvorecký, were sometimes available on the black market. Even Terezín had a jazz band, the 'ghetto swingers', which enjoyed a brief existence before its members were deported to the killing centres in the East.

Sport was popular, although after 1943 increasingly restricted by the demands of war. Ice hockey matches were regularly held at the stadium on the Hetzinsel beneath the Hlávka Bridge. In March 1942, Vienna beat a German team representing Bohemia/Moravia three-nil. Horse racing continued at the Prague track, where black marketeers mingled with film stars, German officers and

ordinary Czechs, attracted by the excitement of the occasion. For those less interested in glamour, there were football matches in the Smíchov stadium. Bicycle races attracted large audiences. These events included novelty indoor competitions at the Lucerna, featuring fixed bicycles on large cylinders which registered the speed of the contestants and the distance they had covered. The collaborationist youth league arranged annual sports galas in Prague every summer which included athletics, canoeing and swimming. These were purely Czech events for the Nazis had learned early on that sporting competitions between Czech and German teams were often used by the crowds to show their resentment of the occupiers. Moreover Czechs must never be seen to defeat Germans, for propaganda about the master race had invested even the result of a football match with political and ideological significance. Goebbels therefore insisted that there must be no competition with Czechs in any area where they might possibly win.

For the majority of the population, the main form of escape from the reality of war was the cinema. Indeed by the end 1944 no other form of entertainment was available in Prague apart from the Apollo Circus. A flourishing Czech film industry existed before the occupation, centred on the studios at Prague-Barrandov. In the 1920s Anny Ondra became an international star as the Czech Mary Pickford, but her career faded with the introduction of sound. In the following decade an Austrian, Hedy Lamarr, created a sensation when she appeared naked in the Czech film *Extase* (*Ecstasy*) of 1933. Despite protests by the Pope,

Wenceslas Square before the blackout restrictions were imposed

Preparation for Hitler's birthday rally in Old Town Square

Extase won a prize at the Venice Film Festival of 1934 and Lamarr ended up in Hollywood. If few Czech stars followed her across the Atlantic, they did establish a European reputation. Amongst the best-known was Lída Baarová, who went to work for UFA in Germany. She had an affair with Goebbels which finally ended in 1938 when his wife threatened divorce and Hitler banned her from the German screen. The Prague movie colony aped the style of Hollywood. The stars lived in luxurious villas with swimming pools near the Barrandov studios or in the smartest suburbs of Prague. A flourishing magazine industry provided the fans with pin-ups, movie news and features on the glittering lifestyle of the top performers, both Czech and American. Local productions filled 20 per cent of the national market with the Germans and the Americans accounting for 33 per cent each. The balance was made up by the British, French and Italians.

The Nazis had no intention of suppressing the Czech film industry although they quickly took a 51 per cent stake in Barrandov where a new German company, Prag-Film, oversaw all aspects of movie production. According to Goebbels, as long as the Czechs avoided 'stupid nationalism' they could play a part in the cinema of the New Europe which would eventually eclipse Hollywood. On 24 March 1939, the magazine *Filmový kurýr* (Film Courier) published an article stating : 'We shall continue our work, for we share the Führer's belief that Prague will flourish and will enjoy long-lasting peace. We also share our President's sincere hope that even within the new form of statehood our nation can realize a peaceful and successful existence and can accomplish great prosperity in the future.' Despite this collaborationist rhetoric, the Czech cinema never made an openly pro-Nazi movie during the war. In the film world, as elsewhere, the Germans imposed censorship and expelled the Jews who were ordered to leave by 15 August 1939. Some, like the actor Hugo Haas, escaped the Holocaust and pursued successful careers in Hollywood. Czech films had to carry German subtitles and a list of restricted topics was issued by the Reichsprotektor's office. Czech films were not allowed to show student life or refer to other groups, such as the Czech Legion, which were considered anti-German. Historical dramas could not criticize the Habsburg Empire. Jews were not to be shown in a positive light. Within these guidelines, the Czech cinema industry continued to operate throughout the war, avoiding open propaganda and concentrating on escapist entertainment. The peak year of production was 1939 when thirty-two Czech feature films were produced. Thereafter production began to shrink with thirty-two movies in 1940 and nineteen in 1941. The last four years of occupation witnessed a further decline with eleven in 1942, eight in 1943 and nine in 1944. Five films were in production when the war ended. Appropriately one of them was entitled *Lavina* (The Avalanche).

American films remained popular in the first two years of the Protectorate but they were eliminated before Pearl Harbor. The last US

The Czech film star Lída Baarová had a notorious pre-war affair with Joseph Goebbels

movie shown in Prague was John Ford's *Stagecoach,* starring John Wayne, which according to regulations imposed by the Nazis, appeared with German sub-titles at the bottom left of the screen and Czech at the bottom right. The première of another western, *Jesse James* starring Henry Fonda and Tyrone Power, was announced but never took place. The gap left by Hollywood was filled by German and to a lesser extent Italian movies. Prague-Barrandov became an important centre of Nazi film making, for it was beyond the range of allied bombers until 1944 and had excellent technical facilities. Goebbels expanded the studio complex, building the largest sound stage in Europe. Amongst the Nazi films produced at Barrandov was the anti-British polemic, *Carl Peters,* starring Hans Albers. The Black extras were provided by over one hundred French colonial troops captured in 1940. Some scenes from the anti-Semitic epic *Jud Süss* (*Jew Süss*) were filmed in Prague and the movie proved highly popular amongst German audiences in the city who cheered and clapped during the final scenes when Süss faces his end. The last Nazi films went into production only months before the final collapse of the Reich. One was *Tiefland,* a movie about mountain climbing, directed by Leni Riefenstahl who later recalled that her relationship with the Czech technicians had been 'amazingly good. Not a word was uttered about war or politics.' The other was

Prague's modern Barrandov film studios were extensively used by the Germans

Goebbels inspecting plans for the expansion of the Barrandov studios

Shiva und die Galgenblume (*Shiva and the Gallows Flower*), loosely based on the Hollywood thriller, *The Maltese Falcon.* It was never completed but the rushes were captured by the Czechs in 1945 and later handed over to the German Communists. They were discovered in a Potsdam vault after the reunification of Germany and finally shown to the public nearly fifty years after the project had begun.

Czech actors, producers and technicians went on working under the occupation. Several changed their names from Czech or Germanized the spelling in deference to the Nazi New Order. But movie stars, like other Czechs, were vulnerable to informers and jealous rivals. The actress Adina Mandlová

was widely rumoured to be Frank's mistress, an accusation she always denied although admitting to wartime affairs with other Germans. At a reception one evening, she was unwise enough to make a joke about Moravec's bald head, a remark that amused his cabinet colleagues and Nazi officials. The Minister of Propaganda, however, never forgave her. At a ball in the Lucerna shortly afterwards, he danced with Mandlová and asked her how she was getting on with Frank. When she replied that she never hung up the phone when Frank called, Moravec secretly denounced her for spreading harmful rumours, an offence that carried the death penalty. The Gestapo took Mandlová from the film set at Barrandov to the Petshek Palace where she was interrogated by Geschke in person. According to the Gestapo chief, Frank was deeply upset by her claim that he was always ringing her. Mandlová was made to sign a declaration stating that she would stop spreading such rumours and denounce anyone who repeated them. Although she was released, she could just as easily have disappeared into a concentration camp. Many on the set were surprised when she returned unharmed.

In 1940, as part of Goebbels grandiose scheme to establish a Nazi movie industry which would rival Hollywood, several Czech stars were asked to take screen tests in German. The only restriction was that they must

Prague-Vysočany after an American bombing raid in 1945

Adina Mandlová, one of the biggest Czech stars was rumoured to have had a relationship with K. H. Frank

A shop sign proclaims: 'Closed for the victory of the Reich'

An official notice in Czech and German threatening looters with death

A sign pointing the way to a public air-raid shelter

A bombed building on the Moldau embankment. The house on the right belonged to the Havel family

A fan magazine cover featuring the Czech 'King of Comedy' Vlasta Burian, who was accused of collaboration after the war

not look too Slav. According to Goebbels, the 'reactionary and chauvinist elements' in the Czech cinema would be destroyed, while 'true patriots' would have the opportunity to serve their country by cooperating with the New Order. Ten Czechs, including Adina Mandlová, were selected for roles in Nazi films. In 1942 Mandlová played opposite Heinz Rühmann in the comedy *Ich vertraue dir meine Frau an* (*I Entrust you, my Wife*). But Hitler disliked stars with Slav names and Goebbels insisted on Mandlová appearing under the more Ayran sounding 'Lil Adina', which she disliked. Meanwhile Frank became involved, demanding that the film should be banned in the Protectorate on the grounds that Mandlová was 'a whore and a chauvinist', an intervention the actress blamed on jealous rivals. In the end she returned to Prague and made no more appearances on the German screen.

The Czech film world continued to live well under the Nazis but it was high society on the edge of the volcano. Like the rest of the population, film stars never knew when an anonymous informer or an incautious remark might lead to a visit from the Gestapo. As a result they lived for the day, never knowing what tomorrow might bring. There was a great deal of heavy drinking which sometimes led to bizarre incidents. At an official reception in the Rudolfinum, the

A chalked sign on a Prague wall proclaims in German: 'We want peace!'

An American air raid on the CKD factory in March 1945

comedian Bedřich Veverka became so drunk that he climbed on to Frank's lap and remarked, 'Hermann – You can call me Fritz.' The embarrassing scene only ended when he was dragged off to sober up. There was also plenty of sex involving Germans as well as Czechs. Mandlová, who was by no means atypical, admitted to a series of war-time affairs and one abortion, procured with the aid of a sympathetic doctor who provided her with a medical certificate calling for a termination. To the ordinary Czech, however, movies meant glamour, and the stars remained the subject of magazines like *Kinorevue* (*Film Review*) which offered readers an escape into a fantasy world of champagne, swimming pools and beautiful women. Wartime reality, however, kept breaking in, with the disappearance of features on Hollywood after 1940 and the sudden, shocking intrusion of a black-bordered official photograph of Heydrich after his death in June 1942. Even in the synthetic wonderland of the movie magazine, there was no escape from the brooding presence of the SS.

Prague was spared the destructive bombing suffered by other major cities during the war. The first raid did not take place until 15 November 1944 when five stray bombs hit a suburban electricity station, killing four and injuring thirty. Although the sirens went off regularly that autumn, the Czechs did not take the threat seriously and were puzzled by the frightened reaction of German refugees from the Ruhr who knew from experience what a major raid would mean. Their mood changed on 14 February 1945, however, when American bombers attacked the city early in the afternoon. The planes appeared from the direction of Jinonice and released a mixed load of high explosive, incendiary and white phosphorous bombs as they passed over the Mozart Bridge. The bridge and many neighbouring buildings were hit, including several hospitals. Amongst the damaged houses was the block on the embankment containing the apartment of the Havel family. A tram on Schwerinstrasse took a direct hit. The raid killed 413 and wounded 1,455. Another eighty-eight were posted missing and presumed dead. By German standards it was a mere nuisance raid, but for the population of Prague, the experience of 'bloody February' was a terrible shock. People became neurotic about bombing. When the sirens sounded some took refuge in the coal cellars of their apartment blocks. Others preferred railway tunnels like the one under the National Museum near the main station which was considered the safest shelter in Prague.

The St Valentine's Day raid had been a tragic error by a few pilots who had lost their way and mistaken the city for Dresden. On 25 March 1945, Ash Wednesday, however, industrial targets, including the Böhmen und Mähren engine works, which was producing self-propelled guns for the Germans, were deliberately attacked. A petrol tank was hit, sending huge clouds of black smoke billowing over the city. The American flyers met little opposition for the flak defences had been stripped by the Germans to support other fronts and the Luftwaffe had been driven from the skies. The death toll from the Ash Wednesday raid was over 500, but the Americans did not come back, despite a series of alerts in the last months of the war. Within weeks of the attack, Hitler was dead and the Russians were in Berlin. Prague, however, the first non-German capital occupied by the Nazis, had still to experience a final episode of bloodshed and destruction before the day of liberation finally dawned.

A greetings card from the last Reichsprotektor Willhelm Frick with best wishes for 1945

> 'Own troops will start an attack at dawn on the south-eastern and southern periphery of the city . . . Many incendiary bombs. The whole nest must burn.'
>
> SS GRUPPENFÜHRER GRAF VON PÜCKLER
> TO FIELD MARSHAL SCHÖRNER,
> 21:50 HOURS, 5 MAY 1945

CHAPTER SEVEN

The Hour Has Come

A German SP gun on fire near Prague's main station

HITLER was determined to hold Bohemia/Moravia with its vital industrial resources. In January 1945, with the Red Army pushing towards the eastern borders of the Protectorate, he placed General Ferdinand Schörner in command of Army Group Centre, which covered a 300-mile front guarding the industrial areas of Silesia and Bohemia/Moravia. Hitler believed that Stalin's main thrust would be towards Prague rather than Berlin and in early April transferred four panzer divisions from the Oder front to Schörner's Army Group. Schörner, promoted Field Marshal in April 1945, was a notorious pro-Nazi, a coarse and brutal man, who stamped out defeatism wherever it emerged. Terror was unleashed on Czechs and Germans alike. On 2 May, when disturbances occurred in the eastern Moravian town of Přerov, Schörner called for 'ruthless action' against 'every hotbed of unrest . . . Participants must be decimated. In the same manner action must be taken against those who are soft and tardy in our own ranks, who fail in this hour.' From trees and bridges in the battle zone dangled the bodies of German soldiers hanged by Schörner's roving court martials. Around the neck of each corpse was a placard stating: 'I am a traitor to the German nation.' In February 1945 Hitler ordered the preparation of 'Fortress Prague'. At the centre of this system was the 'Prague Defence Zone', on the west bank of the Vltava (Moldau) River,

A street barricade at the end of Charles Bridge

A black-bordered newspaper announcing Hitler's death in Berlin

covering the core of Nazi power, the Czernin Palace, the Hradčany Castle and the military installations in Dejvice. Streets leading into this area from the west and north were to be barricaded, the bridges over the Vltava prepared for demolition, and houses on the east bank destroyed to clear a field of fire.

As Nazi Germany entered its death throes, conditions in the Protectorate worsened. Schools did not reopen after the Christmas vacation. The last reserves of labour were rounded up to dig anti-tank ditches. Relations between Czechs and Germans deteriorated as the population looked forward to the day of liberation. A German film actor recalled that in early 1945 the atmosphere became icy. He was frightened enough to barricade the door of his hotel room at night. According to a Swedish journalist, things were so tense that the 'least spark might result in a violent explosion'. Partisan bands became active in early 1945 as a wave of parachute groups was dropped by the Russians to encourage disruption behind the Nazi lines. They were responsible for a series of attacks on troop trains and rail bridges in March and April. A few parachutists were also dropped by the British Special Operations Executive (SOE), operating from Bari in Italy. The German security police established special battle groups to deal with this threat, while the Gestapo tried to penetrate the resistance networks that supported the partisans. Savage reprisals were taken against anyone suspected of helping parachutists or sabotaging the German war effort.

Pulling down German signs in the streets of Prague

The resistance prepared for a final blow against the tottering occupation regime. In April 1945 a Czech National Committee (ČNR) was formed representing both Communists and non-Communists. The chairman of the ČNR was an academic, Professor

Czech crowds burning German propaganda books

Albert Pražák of Charles University, and his deputy, the Communist Josef Smrkovský. Beneš had a liaison officer, Captain Jaromír Nechanský, with the ČNR to maintain radio contact with London. On 23 April the government in exile, now established behind the Russian lines at Košice in Slovakia, broadcast an appeal to the nation, calling for a general strike and an uprising against the Nazis: 'Now the moment has come to repay the Germans for all those who have died a terrible death at German hands, for the sufferings of the imprisoned, the humiliation of the enslaved, and for the tears and sorrows of the countless unhappy families of our nation.' The Nazi radio replied with a threat to destroy Prague. The city was German, a bastion of European civilization against the Bolshevik hordes. German soldiers would defend it until the last round. Despite this rhetoric, however, nobody wanted a prolonged battle in Prague. The Nazis needed peace and order behind Army Group Centre. The resistance did not envisage heavy fighting but a coup against an already defeated enemy which would be quickly supported by allied forces.

On 25 April the German Army commander, General Toussaint, called a state of alert in

Prague. In the event of trouble he could count on little assistance from Army Group Centre which was fully committed against the Russians in eastern Moravia. The city itself was garrisoned by administrative troops, a few security police (Gestapo and SD) under SS Standartenführer Dr Erwin Weinmann, and around 1000 uniformed police (Ordnungspolizei) under SS Gruppenführer Paul Geibel. In an emergency, however, reinforcements could be summoned from outside Prague. There was an army tank training centre at Milovice, forty kilometers north-east of Prague. Various SS units were also available. The Waffen SS commander, Gruppenführer Karl-Friedrich von Puckler, could call on the 'Der Führer' Regiment of the 2nd SS Panzer Division 'Das Reich', under Obersturmbannführer Otto Weidinger, which had retreated into the Protectorate after the fall of Vienna. Based at Litoměřice, seventy-five kilometers north-west of Prague, 'Der Führer' was short of fuel but had tanks and could be relied upon to fight. Von Pückler had also raised his own ersatz PanzerGrenadier Regiment, 'Kampfgruppe Wallenstein' from SS recruits and training cadres at the Benešov exercise area, thirty kilometers south-east of Prague. 'Wallenstein' had a few Tiger tanks and some artillery. At Ruzyně airfield, eight kilometers west of the city, the Luftwaffe had established a huge holding centre for its remaining aircraft. Many were unable to fly for lack of spares and fuel but enough remained to form a reinforced fighter squadron, 'Gefechtsverband Hogeback', with Messerschmit 262 jets.

The Germans, however, like the Czech resistance, wanted to avoid trouble in the last days of the war. Prague was a vital communications centre behind Schörner's Army Group. It had to be held until German civilians had been evacuated from the path of the Red Army and Schörner's troops had made a fighting retreat towards the American lines. But there was no thought of a heroic last stand amidst the ruins. As a fortress, Prague existed only in Hitler's imagination. By the time of his suicide in Berlin on 30 April nothing had been done about the defence of the city beyond preparing the Vltava bridges

Czechs replacing the Nazi eagle with the Czech lion on the former German Opera House while two Ordnungspolizei look on

Czech crowds booing at an SS car in Wenceslas Square

for demolition. Since early spring, Frank had been seeking a political solution to the impending crisis in the Protectorate. Like many of the Nazi leaders he hoped for a break between the Western allies and the Russians which would enlist the Anglo-Americans in the struggle against Bolshevism. This would save his own people, the Sudetens, from the consequences of defeat and preserve German influence in the Czech lands. He hoped to split the resistance by exploiting the anti-Communism of the Czech middle class, and to work through collaborators in the Protectorate government. On 4 April 1945, Frank saw Hitler for the last time and requested permission to send a Czech delegation to the Americans who would be offered a peaceful occupation of Bohemia/Moravia. Hitler refused, claiming that new 'wonder weapons', V-2 rockets and schnorkel U-boats, would soon reverse the whole course of the war.

Despite this response Frank did not abandon his plan. He returned to Prague where he tried to contact the Americans through the International Red Cross and the Vatican. He also enlisted the help of Hitler's Minister of Armaments, Albert Speer, who opposed the Führer's policy of scorched earth and resistance to the last round. On 23 April 1945, with the US 3rd Army under General George

A Czech policeman confonts a German patrol near Old Town Square

Prague Radio Station was at the very heart of the uprising

S. Patton already entering the Sudetenland, Frank was informed by Speer that Hitler had finally been persuaded to agree to his scheme. The Nazi Foreign Minister, Ribbentrop, visiting Hitler's bunker for the last time, had also approved. A Czech delegation flew to Munich the next day. Although the Americans refused to talk to these collaborators, Frank did not give up. Instead he tried unsuccessfully to persuade prominent members of the non-Communist resistance, incarcerated in the 'Small Fortress' at Terezín, to join a reconstructed Czech government. These men were Frank's personal insurance policy, saved from death because he thought they might be useful one day. None, however, was prepared to join the sinking ship, despite the inducements offered by Frank's personal representative, Willi Leimer of the Prague Gestapo.

Three days after Hitler's suicide, Frank was summoned to Flensburg near the Danish border for a meeting with the Führer's designated successor, Grand Admiral Karl Dönitz. Frank argued that a revolution in the Protectorate could not be long delayed. He proposed handing over political power to a reorganized Protectorate government which would then invite the Americans into Bohemia/Moravia. This would preserve order behind the lines and allow Schörner to continue fighting. Dönitz and his chief of staff, General Alfred Jodl, had still not lost hope of driving a wedge between the Western allies and the Russians. At the very least they hoped to conclude a separate armistice which would allow time for the retreat of German troops and civilians from the East. Frank's plan fitted into this overall strategy and was quickly approved. On the evening of 3 May, Hamburg Radio announced that Prague had been declared 'a hospital city'.

The International Red Cross would assume responsibility for wounded and prisoners of war. Negotiations for 'a political reorganization' had already begun. Any attempt to interfere with this process would 'lead to Bolshevist chaos' and would be suppressed 'by force of arms'. The Russians offered not liberation but 'Bolshevization'. The following morning Frank left Flensburg and flew to Schörner's HQ in Hradec Králové to brief him on the plan. He arrived back in Prague in the early hours of 5 May with full power to form a new Czech government and to send an emissary to General Eisenhower. This initiative, however, was rapidly overtaken by events.

Although the troops of Patton's Third US Army had entered the Sudetenland on 18 April, it was no part of American strategy to occupy the Protectorate. The main thrust of Patton's advance was towards Austria and Bavaria to pre-empt the creation of a mythical Nazi Alpine redoubt. As the Supreme Allied Commander, General Dwight D. Eisenhower informed the British Prime Minister, Winston Churchill, on 23 April, he 'had never conceived of Prague as a military, still less as a political objective'. With enemy resistance collapsing, however, the question of Bohemia/Moravia assumed increasing

Bodies of civilians caught in the crossfire near the Radio Station

A German arrested by Czech fighters

Czech fighters with a captured German policeman

significance. Concerned by Stalin's obvious determination to impose his own solutions in Poland, Churchill pressed for a US advance on Prague to increase the bargaining power of the Western allies and limit Soviet influence in East/Central Europe. But the Americans were reluctant. The US Chief of Staff, General George Marshall, had no desire to waste lives unnecessarily or to challenge the Russians whose participation in the war against Japan remained a US priority. The matter was left up to General Eisenhower, who refused to subordinate military operations to political considerations. On 4 May Patton was authorized to make a limited advance into Czechoslovakia, halting at the line Karlovy Vary–Plzeň–Budějovice. A drive towards the Vltava valley and Prague would be undertaken only with the agreement of the Russians. When Eisenhower raised this possibility on 4 May, however, the Soviet High Command reacted quickly, emphasizing the need to avoid 'a possible confusion of forces'. Deferring to Russian wishes, Eisenhower ordered Patton to stop at Plzeň. As Orme Sargent of the Foreign Office informed Churchill on 6 May : 'I am afraid this means that General Eisenhower has pledged himself *not* to go to Prague.'

The Germans and the British were not alone in desiring an American advance. President Beneš, established with his exile government

The cavalry of General Vlasov's Russian National Liberation Army entering Prague

The insignia of the Russian National Liberation Army

A Vlasov soldier guarding German prisoners

A group of Vlasov soldiers in the Košíře district of Prague

in Košice, was also looking forward to the arrival of Patton. Despite his deference to Stalin throughout the war and his readiness to grant the Communists a leading role in his government, Beneš was experiencing the reality of Soviet power for the first time. Not only did Stalin annexe Ruthenia after a spurious plebiscite but he also cut Beneš off from all contact with the West. US and

Barricades were hurriedly constructed after an appeal by Prague Radio

On the corner of Old Town Square, Czechs take cover from the firing

British diplomats were not allowed to follow the President to Košice where he was kept isolated by the Red Army. According to his personal secretary, Eduard Táborský, when Beneš heard that the Americans were in the Sudetenland, he exclaimed : ' "Thank God, Thank God." Unable to contain his excitement he began to pace his study, and to judge by the expression in his eyes he was already visualizing the beneficial political consequences of this event.' Non-Communist elements in the Czech resistance also hoped for help from the West. In November 1944 and again in January 1945 the Prague underground begged SOE to send more arms to counter the growing power and prestige of the Communists : 'If partisans are to be supplied with arms and equipment only from the East as has been the case so far, then the influence of the East will be overwhelming.' The Czechs, however, were not a British priority and the necessary aircraft were never available. As the war drew to a close the resistance was thus split, despite the façade of unity offered by the ČNR. The Communists hoped for the liberation of Prague by the Red Army. The non-Communists awaited the arrival of Patton. Both were aware of the implications for the future of Czechoslovakia.

Stalin, who had always combined war with politics, never intended to abandon the Czech capital to the Americans. Soviet intelligence kept him well informed about Frank's plans and Churchill's pressure on Washington. In order to pre-empt a possible alignment between the Anglo-Americans and non-Communist forces in Bohemia/Moravia, he insisted that Russian plans for an advance on Prague must be brought forward. He had displayed a similar determination to take Budapest and Berlin no matter what the cost in the lives of his soldiers. With Hitler dead and the German capital in Russian hands, Prague

became the prime Soviet objective. On 1 May 1945, Marshal Koniev's 1st Ukrainian Front was ordered to wheel away from Berlin and advance west of Dresden along both banks of the Vltava towards Prague. The next day Marshal Malinovski's 2nd Ukrainian Front, which had just captured Brno, was ordered to move on Prague from the south-west, swinging inwards on the left flank of Marshal A. I. Yeremenko's 4th Ukrainian Front and cutting off Schörner's Army Group Centre in Moravia. The Soviet offensive was to begin on 7 May and take the Czech capital within six days. These US and Soviet decisions were unknown to Dönitz and Frank. The Czech resistance was also unaware that the Americans were not coming. Thus on the eve of the rising the judgements of the main protagonists in Prague were based on false assumptions.

Besides the American, Soviet and German armies, there was another force on the territory of Bohemia/Moravia which was shortly to play an important role in the fate of Prague. This was the 1st Division of Vlasov's Russian National Liberation Army under General Sergei K. Bunyachenko which suddenly appeared north of the city in early May. Thrown into the fighting on the Eastern front, the 1st Division had withdrawn from the line around Frankfurt-an-der-Oder at the end of April 1945 and marched into the Protectorate, refusing to accept orders from General Schörner. Nobody, least of all his SS liaison officers, knew what Bunyachenko intended to do. Vlasov, called in by the Germans to control his subordinate, acted with deliberate ambiguity, leaving Bunyachenko to act as he thought fit. On 2 May, near Kozojed, the Russians were approached by representatives of the Czech resistance in Prague led by an unknown police colonel. According to one of Bunyachenko's officers,

Barricades were built throughout the city

Lieutenant-Colonel Artemev, the Czechs revealed that they were preparing an uprising in the city and requested the assistance of the 1st Division. A possible deal was suggested. If Bunyachenko helped the Czechs against the Germans, the Czechs would offer his troops political asylum from the advancing Soviet forces. It was a bargain based partly on desperation and partly on the anti-Communism of both sides.

Although the Czech National Committee planned an uprising, it was still biding its time. The Communists, who were preparing a general strike, instructed party cells to stay calm and await instructions. Another group, the secret army of the non-Communist ON, under General František Slunéčko (Codename 'Alex'), had created a Prague military command based on the police and the Protectorate guard. On 30 April 1945, Slunéčko named General Karel Kutlvašr (Codename 'Bartoš') as battle commandant of the city. Two days later Kutlvašr secretly inspected the Prague radio station which was to give the signal for the uprising and arranged for the preparation of back-up transmitters at other locations. His plans, however, had not been cleared with the military command of the ČNR which was headed by the Communist, Václav David. But these preparations were rapidly overtaken by events. Late on 1 May, Dönitz spoke on the radio announcing Hitler's death. The text was published next morning, when the Prague newspapers appeared with heavy black mourning borders. A mood of expectation swept the city. On 3 May the population began to take matters into its own hands.

In some areas German street signs were torn down. Despite threats by the German controlled radio and the street loudspeaker system, and a show of force by German jets which screamed low over the city, trouble escalated the next day. The Ministry of Transport began to remove German signs from stations and post offices. Tram conductors refused to accept Reichsmarks or announce the stops in German. German soldiers were mobbed and disarmed. Allied flags appeared in windows. In the suburb of Vršovice, a Red Cross centre for concentration-camp victims was surrounded by a large crowd which sang the national anthem and tore up a swastika flag. A German policeman from the nearby Ordnungspolizei barracks was shot dead by a Czech gendarme when he tried to intervene. The firing caused panic and the crowd scattered. In the confusion a Czech policeman shot and fatally wounded a second man in plain clothes. He was carrying German identity papers and was thought to be a Gestapo agent. Despite his pleas for help the wounded man was left to bleed to death on the pavement. Ironically he was a member of the Communist underground on his way to a secret meeting. There were scattered incidents in other suburbs and a huge crowd gathered in Wenceslas Square. It was into this atmosphere of expectation and intrigue that Frank returned on the evening of 4 May.

While Frank was visiting Dönitz, the Protectorate government had decided it could wait no longer. On 28 April Hácha sent a final birthday greeting to Hitler, pledging that the people of Bohemia/Moravia would fight

Czech medical teams rescuing the wounded

to the death alongside their Führer, but his ministers were already trying to save their own skins. On 4 May they drew up a memorandum demanding that the Germans turn over power to a reconstructed cabinet led by Dr Richard Bienert, the Minister of the Interior, which would proclaim the end of the Protectorate. At 11:00 on 5 May a delegation arrived at the Czernin Palace to present these demands. At 13:30 talks began between Bienert, Frank and Toussaint. By then, however, events had begun to overtake both parties to the negotiations. At 06:00 the Prague radio station on Schwerinstrasse, behind the National Museum, announced the time in Czech and broadcast only in Czech thereafter. Czech flags began to appear on the public buildings and the last German signs were torn down. In the Old Town and Vinohrady, German police patrols tried to force shopkeepers to put the signs back, smashing the windows of those who refused. At 10:50 a strong force of Ordnungspolizei set up machine guns in front of the National Museum and advanced into Wenceslas Square, forcing the crowds into the side streets. Another detachment moved up Schwerinstrasse to the radio station and occupied the lower floors. At 12:45 the staff, barricaded in the studios, began to broadcast desperate appeals to the people of Prague :

An American patrol brings a German staff officer to Prague with news of the unconditional surrender signed at Reims

An American patrol in the streets of Prague

The German military commander arriving at Prague Police Headquarters to negotiate a ceasefire

'We request the Czech police, all Czech soldiers and all Czechs to come to the radio building immediately. We need help.'

At 11:00 the Protectorate guard at Štefánik Barracks in Smíchov rebelled, taking an oath of allegiance to the Beneš government in Košice. An hour later the police went over to the uprising. A strong force was despatched from the police headquarters on Bartolomäeusgasse to raise the siege of Prague Radio. Fighting began all over the city centre. The Ordnungspolizei abandoned Wenceslas Square, withdrawing to the National Museum and the main station. As the shooting intensified an unknown woman walked through the crossfire to the Wenceslas statue where she knelt in prayer. At the radio station there was heavy fighting between Czech police and the Germans inside the building, who were supported by a Wehrmacht post on Humboldtstrasse which commanded the side entrance. The attackers were reinforced in the afternoon by troops of the Protectorate guard from Smíchov who advanced across the roofs of neighbouring buildings and entered the radio station through the upper stories. By 16:00, after a murderous struggle in darkened corridors and stairwells, the Ordnungspolizei had been forced into the cellars where they surrendered. The army post on Humboldtstrasse also capitulated after two escaped British prisoners of war assured the garrison that their lives would be spared. By this time the Czechs held not only the main radio station, but also the street loudspeaker system controlled from the Old Town Hall and the main telephone exchange at Žižkov. The Czech Press Agency, ČTK, had established direct contact with Reuters. Of the communications facilities in the Prague area, only the transmitter at Liblice remained in German hands, broadcasting programmes prepared by Schörner's intelligence section.

Kutlvašr, surprised by the fighting, spent the morning trying to obtain orders from Slunéčko, dodging from one hiding place to another through the lethal confusion of the streets. But Slunéčko was not in the city. Unable to make contact, Kutlvašr went to the police presidium on Bartolomäeusgasse at 14:00 where he assumed command of the uprising, directing the fighting through the police communications system. Around the same time the ČNR met hurriedly in Ziegengasse, off Old Town Square, and

attempted to assert its political control, proclaiming itself the legal representative of the government in Košice. In the middle of the developing chaos, the first Americans reached Prague - an OSS (Office of Strategic Services) jeep patrol led by Lieutenant Eugene Fodor. It remains unclear what Fodor was doing in Prague but he was immediately taken first to the police presidium and then to the ČNR building off Old Town Square. It was agreed that he should return immediately to the American lines near Plzeň and request an advance on Prague. He left late that afternoon, taking Nechanský with him as a representative of the ČNR. The appearance of Fodor's jeep encouraged people to believe that their long ordeal was over and that the Americans were about to liberate the city.

If the uprising had taken the resistance by surprise, it had also upset Frank's plans. In the afternoon German planes dropped leaflets over the city announcing that the government had been handed over to Bienert and requesting the maintenance of order until the Americans arrived. In fact this

German shells set fire to buildings in Old Town Square

information had long since been overtaken by events. As news of the disturbances in the city below reached the Czernin Palace, Frank suspended talks with the Protectorate ministers to allow Bienert to report progress to the Czech people and issue an appeal for calm over the radio. At the same time Frank sent a delegation, consisting of Toussaint's chief of staff, General Ziervogel, and the Minister of Labour, Bertsch, to contact the Americans. Bienert was unable to reach the broadcasting station because of the fighting on Schwerinstrasse. Deciding to use the street loudspeaker system instead, he made his way to the Old Town Hall where he was promptly arrested by the insurgents. Brought before the ČNR, he acknowledged its legal authority, killing off Frank's plan to install a government of collaborators. As for Frank's delegation to Patton, it was arrested by partisans west of Kladno and never reached the American lines.

By the evening of 5 May, most of Prague east of the river was in Czech hands with the exception of Gestapo headquarters at the

Petschek Palace, the main railway station, the tank school building in Žižkov, the barracks at Karlín, and the SS base in the former Law Faculty of Charles University near the Mendel Bridge. In a message to Army Group Centre at 20:15, the Waffen SS commander, von Pückler, reported that the military position was unclear: 'Considerable casualties in action as we are under fire from every house ... Assessment of the situation only possible when we know the result of the planned advance on May 6. The insurgents are fighting unexpectedly well and spiritedly.' Although ordinary German soldiers had shown little stomach for battle, the SS was a different proposition. That afternoon the first atrocities occurred when SS troops shot hostages on the Mendel Bridge. In other areas of the city, Czechs hunted down German civilians accused of sniping from the roofs. Some were thrown from high windows. Others were hung upside down from lampposts and set on fire. The lucky ones were often beaten and kicked before being forced into air-raid shelters where they were detained without food or water. Women and children were also roughly treated. After six years of occupation, the population was in no mood to distinguish ordinary Germans from Nazi fanatics.

At 21:00 negotiations began between Frank and the ČNR, with the assistance of the International Red Cross. Frank was prepared to hand over political power to the Czechs if they abandoned their military positions, surrendered their weapons and freed all German prisoners. In a parallel set of talks with the Prague military command, the head of the Nazi security police, Weinmann, stated that the ČNR could be recognized as the representative of the Czech people but must first cease all attacks on German installations and refrain from interfering with the movement of arms and supplies to Army Group Centre. The Waffen SS commander, von Pückler, took a harsher line in a telephone conversation with Kutlvašr at 02:30, emphasizing that Frank would talk about an autonomous regime only if the Czechs gave up their positions, surrendered their weapons and rearmed their German prisoners. This amounted to a demand for a complete capitulation which would have left the city at the mercy of the SS.

Both sides were trying to gain time. The Germans had summoned units from outside the city and hoped to improve their military position next day. The uprising threatened the planned retreat of Army Group Centre and endangered the strategy agreed at Flensburg. When the talks began on the evening of 5 May, the first reinforcements were already arriving, SS 'Kampfgruppe Wallenstein' advancing on Smíchov and Pankrác along both sides of the Vltava River. The column on the right bank had reached Krč where it halted for the night. Other units were slower. Kampfgruppe Milovice, from the army tank training school north-east of Prague, was delayed by lack of fuel. 'Der Führer' at Litoměrice was too far outside the city to intervene immediately and its movement was impeded by partisans. In a report to Army Group Centre von Pückler defined the aim of the operation next day as clearing the Old Town and the area of Wenceslas Square with the support of the Luftwaffe: 'Own troops will start attack at dawn on the south-eastern and southern periphery of the city from the direction of Beneschau [Benešov] along the right bank, and from the direction of Königsaal [Zbraslav], along the left bank of the Moldau [Vltava] towards the north. Note swastikas on houses and red crosses on buildings and visual markings for the airforce ... Many incendiary bombs. The whole nest must burn.' In a later message he declared: 'We are politically and militarily determined. Goal: Reckless action in support of the Reich and the secure restoration of German supremacy.' Meanwhile the Czechs, short of weapons and ammunition, were waiting for the Americans to arrive, and tried to avoid provocation. As a result there was a ceasefire on the night of 5/6 May, broken only by a few isolated incidents including a German attack on the National Bank.

The Czechs at first believed that the SS units advancing on Prague were American troops. The tanks at Krč were known to be German, but it was assumed that they had halted to surrender. The ČNR sent an officer to the area to negotiate the capitulation. The truth only became clear late on 5 May, when the ČNR concluded that the Germans intended to fight and appealed through the radio for the population to barricade the streets. All over the city trams were overturned and cobblestones ripped up. There was little military planning in this activity which was carried out at random by crowds of people acting on their own. In the early hours of the morning calls for help were broadcast to the allies both in English and Russian requesting arms drops and air support. Street lights were

illuminated in certain areas to define dropping zones for paratroops and arms supplies. At 03:28 Prague Radio also begged the Russian National Liberation Army to intervene. In fact Bunyachenko had already made his decision. On the evening of 5 May, he interned his SS liaison officers and ordered his division, which had reached Beroun, twenty kilometers south-west of Prague, to march on the city. The Russians advanced in three columns. The 1st Regiment, under Lieutenant-Colonel Archipov, moved on the right flank through Liteň towards the suburb of Radotín. In the centre the 2nd Regiment under Lieutenant-Colonel Artemev thrust through Kuchař towards Jinonice. On the left the 3rd Regiment under Lieutenant-Colonel Aleksandrov-Rybcov and the 4th Regiment commanded by Colonel Sacharov, advanced down the Beroun–Prague road. In order to avoid confusion, the Russians fastened tricolours in white, blue and red to their German-style uniforms.

On the morning of 6 May, Bunyachenko established his headquarters at Jinonice. In

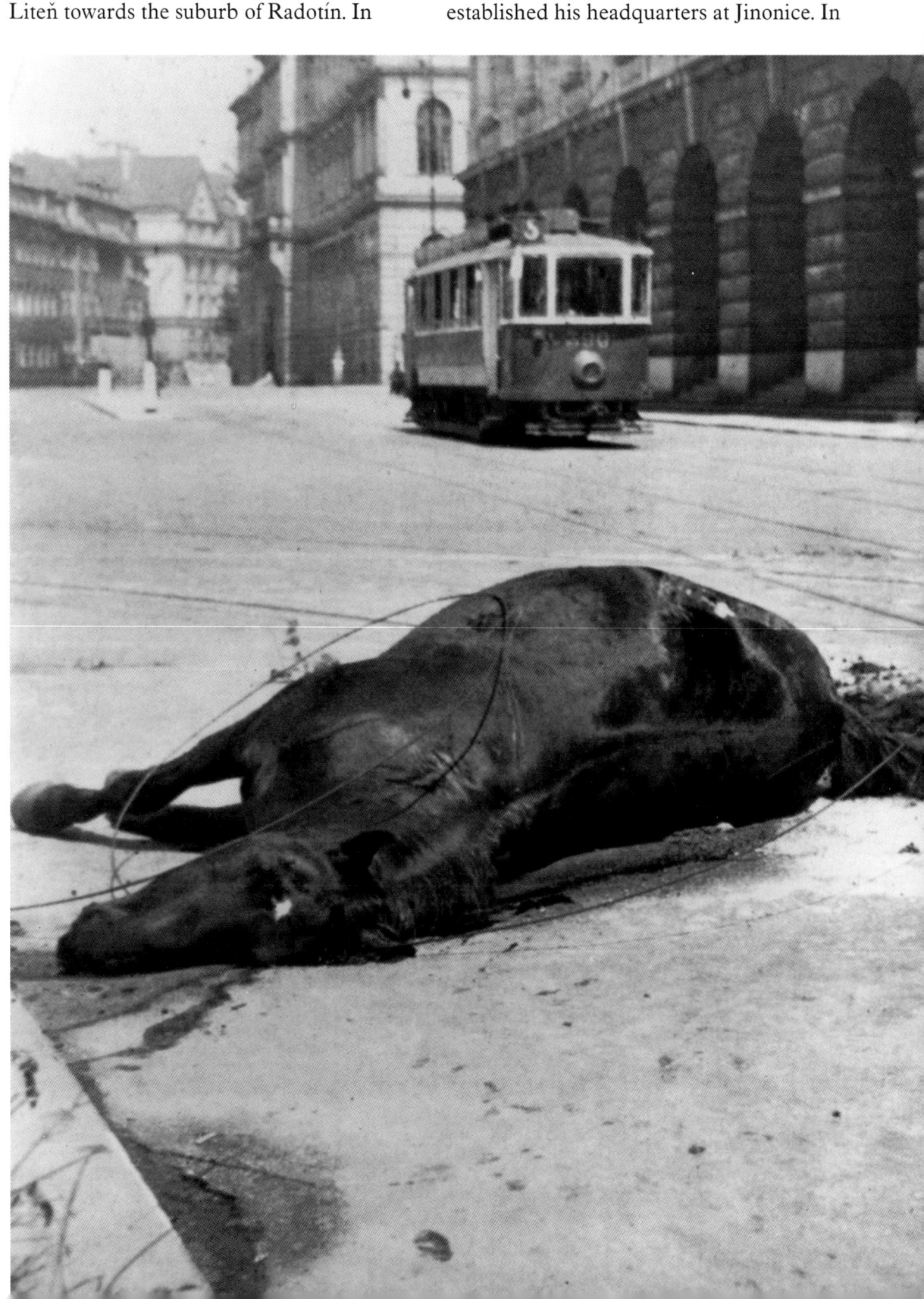

Aftermath of the fighting around the Rudolfinum and the SS barracks at Charles University Law School

the streets the Russians were greeted as heroes by crowds of Czechs who cheered the marching columns and opened a way through the barricades. At 10:00 a message arrived from the reconnaisance section under Major Kostenko, that he was under attack by an SS force with six Tiger tanks in the suburb of Zbraslav. This was in fact part of Kampfgruppe Wallenstein advancing on the left bank of the Vltava. Bunyachenko immediately ordered Archipov's 1st Regiment, moving up from Korno, to support Kostenko. In a surprise attack the Russians forced the SS to retreat across the river and secured the bridges between Zbraslav and Chuchle. They also occupied the high ground around the village of Slivenec which commanded Prague and access from the east to the Plzeň road. There was heavy fighting for this objective which the Germans west of the Vltava had to control, either to break into Prague or if necessary to reach the Plzeň road and the safety of the American lines. In the afternoon, the 3rd Regiment surrounded Ruzyně airfield, which was regarded by the Czech military command as a vital objective, not

Laying out Prague's dead

only because its capture would deprive the Germans of air support but also because in Czech hands the base could be used by allied aircraft bringing arms and reinforcements.

The chief of staff of VIII Fliegerkorps, Colonel Sorge, who knew Vlasov and had helped him organize a Russian air squadron, believed that there had been a misunderstanding. He left Ruzyně under a flag of truce to settle matters by negotiation. His adjutant soon returned, however, to say that unless decided to attack the Russian columns with every available aircraft. Since the 3rd Regiment commanded the runway with artillery, however, the Germans could not land to rearm and refuel. The remaining jets flew to Zatec in western Bohemia, abandoning Ruzyně as an operational base. The only airfield still in German hands was the small satellite field at Bohnice on the north bank of the Vltava. By 23:00 on 6 May, the 1st Division was deployed in a curved line from Ruzyně through Břevnov and Smíchov, then along the left bank of the Vltava to Zbraslav,

A German delegation on its way to conclude a ceasefire at Prague Police HQ

the airfield surrendered immediately, Sorge would be shot. When capitulation did not follow, the Russians carried out their threat. First Lieutenant Buschmann, despatched from Havlíčkův Brod in a light aircraft by the commander of VIII Fliegerkorps, General Seidemann, to contact Vlasov and resolve the situation, was shot down and wounded south of Ruzyně. As negotiations failed and it became clear that these events were part of a wider operation, the Germans driving a wedge between the German forces converging on the city.

While the Russian National Liberation Army engaged the SS, the Czechs continued to await the arrival of the Americans. Fodor had contacted advance patrols of General Hubner's V Corps near Plzeň on the evening of 5 May and news of the uprising was immediately passed up the chain of command to Patton. A ruthless and ambitious commander,

Patton wanted the distinction of liberating the last European capital still in Nazi hands and pressed Eisenhower to waive his halt order. Relaying this request through General Bradley, Patton suggested that he should be allowed to 'create facts', deliberately losing contact with higher headquarters while the advance continued. The next time he contacted Bradley would be from a phone booth in Wenceslas Square. The following morning V Corps took Plzeň and halted to await orders. The Germans were eager to surrender, marching to the prisoner of-war compounds without guards or driving into captivity in their own trucks. The Czechs greeted the Americans with wild enthusiasm. As one correspondent reported, it was just like the liberation of Paris with 'wine, flowers and kisses'. The troops were 'delighted to have resumed the role of liberators and to be in a country where fraternization is not only no crime but a pleasing accompaniment of these last days of battle'.

At this point another Czech emissary arrived from Prague, Police Inspector Jaroslav Ženatý, who had been despatched by Pražák to reinforce Fodor's appeal. Ženatý had made the journey to Plzeň by motorbike, wearing a Red Cross helmet and armband as a flimsy protection against air attack. He was quizzed by US intelligence officers about the disposition of German forces, possible routes into the city and the condition of the bridges over the Vltava. Ženatý returned to Prague convinced that the Americans were coming to the rescue. His news was welcomed by Pražák but Smrkovský was less pleased, listening 'stonefaced' to Ženatý's report. The Communists had not been informed about Ženatý's mission and hoped that the Red Army would liberate the city. But the die had already been cast. On the morning of 6 May, Bradley phoned Patton with the news that the stop line was mandatory : 'You must not – I repeat *not* reconnoitre to a greater depth than five miles north-east of Pilsen [Plzeň]. Ike does not want any international complications at this late date.' The halt order applied not only to 3rd Army but to the small Czech unit which had been attached to the Americans on 21 April to provide a symbolic presence on liberated soil. As one of the soldiers later recalled : 'On May 1 we entered Czech territory near Cheb. On May 7 we liberated Plzeň. American officers stopped our further advance at Rokycany. They refused to let us continue ... because, as they said, there had been an agreement between the Great Powers that this area was to be liberated by Soviet troops.' Ironically, the Germans would not have resisted a drive on Prague. At 14:12 on 6 May, Dönitz ordered his forces in the Protectorate to open their lines to the Americans.

Czech appeals for help also reached London both from public broadcasts monitored by the BBC and over a direct radio link with Nechanský who was in touch with Beneš' representative in Britain, Hubert Ripka. The Chiefs of Staff and SOE had never encouraged the Czechs to hope for British assistance in the event of an uprising and had made their views 'absolutely clear' to Beneš

before he left for Košice. They were, however, prepared to drop emergency supplies to the insurgents and twenty-four Halifax bombers were allocated for this purpose. But on the afternoon of 6 May, the RAF cancelled the mission. No reason was given but it was probably because the stop line laid down by Eisenhower applied equally to air operations. As with a land advance, an air supply drop would have been unopposed by the Germans for the flak defences of Prague had been redeployed. Thereafter the British merely forwarded Czech messages to Eisenhower, who in turn sent them on to Moscow. Stalin responded by bringing forward

A Czech magazine cover celebrates the barricade fighters

the date of the Soviet offensive by one day. He wanted Koniev in Prague before the desperate military situation forced the Americans to intervene. In fact there was little danger of this. On 6 May, the day the Soviet attack began, General Jodl flew to Reims to discuss unconditional surrender. Eisenhower hoped that a German capitulation on all fronts would save Prague, ending the pressure for Western intervention.

It was against this background that a new round of talks began between the Germans and the ČNR on 6 May in the offices of the International Red Cross. Frank's representatives, Weinmann and Leimer, stated that he would hand over power to the ČNR provided that Schörner could continue to fight the Red Army. If this was agreed, Frank would declare the capital an open city and suspend all troop movements until the arrival of the allies. This compromise was strongly opposed by David, Smrkovský and other committee members. Beneš' military liaison officer with the ČNR, Captain Nechanský, ignorant of developments at Eisenhower's headquarters, pointed out that the Americans were a mere fifty kilometers away and that London would send arms. In reality, however, the German military position remained strong. Kampfgruppe Wallenstein, although repelled by Bunyachenko at Slivenec and Zbraslav on the west bank of the Vltava, had reached Pankrác and occupied the high ground in Michle to the east. Der Führer, delayed at Chabry by partisans, entered the suburb of Prague-Kobylisy around midnight and prepared to move through Libeň towards the Troja Bridge. The Milovice group was still experiencing fuel problems but was expected to attack the next day. Although von Pückler informed Schörner of heavy fighting with elements of the Russian Liberation Army, he believed this was the result of a misunderstanding with Vlasov. He still hoped to put down the uprising when reinforcements were committed to the battle. As the fighting entered its third day, Czech prospects hung in the balance.

At 05:00 on 7 May, Bunyachenko's troops renewed their attack. The 1st Regiment took the Železniční, Mozart and Dienzenhofer

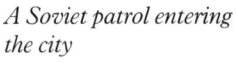
A Soviet patrol entering the city

Jubilant Czechs welcome a Soviet tank on a Prague street

Bridges, blocking the advance of Kampfgruppe Wallenstein and reaching Vinohrady, Strašnice and Pankrác by the afternoon. In the eastern suburbs it engaged German reinforcements moving into Prague. Elements of the Milovice battle group reached the main railway station and Republic Square but were unable to make any further progress. Bunyachenko's 3rd and 4th Regiments attacked objectives on the Petřín Hill. In the Holešovice area Der Führer attempted to cross the Vltava from Libeň but was halted by barricades. Russian artillery shelled Nazi positions in the city.

The Germans, still unable to believe that their allies had really turned against them, tried to negotiate a ceasefire. In a letter to Bunyachenko, the German army commander, General Toussaint, emphasized their common struggle against Bolshevism and called for an end to the fighting. He expressed his determination to crush the Czech rebellion which he implied was inspired by Communism. These appeals were brushed aside. According to a proclamation by Bunyachenko, the Germans must surrender to the Russian Liberation Army or face total destruction.

Although he was unable to carry out this threat, by the end of the afternoon Bunyachenko had prevented the Germans from crushing the centre of the uprising in the Old Town and left the Czechs free to deal with remaining German strong points there. In the process his troops had taken over 500 prisoners for the Germans were more willing to surrender to uniformed and disciplined Russians than to Czech irregulars. Bunyachenko claimed to have suffered 300 casualties although this figure may have been exaggerated for political purposes in negotiations with the ČNR. As the fighting intensified the SS resorted to desperate measures, shooting hostages if road blocks were not cleared, setting fire to apartment buildings and driving Czechs in front of their tanks. In Pankrác small children were dragged out of air-raid shelters and

Soviet troops in Wenceslas Square

Red Army troops are welcomed by a Czech girl in a traditional folk costume. Such pictures were soon exploited for their propaganda value

bayoneted. The Czechs retaliated by shooting prisoners and tying captured Germans to their barricades. Without the intervention of the Russians, Prague might have shared the fate of Warsaw for Schörner was determined to destroy the city if necessary and von Pückler was quite capable of carrying out his orders.

Bunyachenko's military success was not matched by political progress. Although the intervention of his division was vital, its presence in Prague was a political embarrassment. The ČNR was not a party to his agreement with resistance representatives and no group was prepared to say that it had authorized the deal. In this situation, friction began almost immediately. The Czechs refused to broadcast Bunyachenko's ultimatum to Frank. In talks with Bunyachenko's liaison officer, Captain Antonov, the ČNR insisted that the Germans could surrender only to the national committee as the legal representative of the Czechoslovak government. The committee also cut off

Wenceslas Square after the fighting

Captured Germans are forced to clear a barricade while a hostile crowd looks on

A German officer hanging from a lamp-post on a Prague street

Bunyachenko's access to the radio. When a Prague announcer stated that the Russian Liberation Army was in negotiation with the ČNR, he was immediately removed. Even this was considered too risky. In the afternoon a ČNR delegation under the Communist, David, reached a four-point agreement with the Russians on military cooperation but Antonov concluded that while the Czechs wanted the armed intervention of the 1st Division, they were unwilling to pay a political price. The agreement on asylum was no longer valid.

While the debate about the Russians continued in the ČNR, events occurred which profoundly affected the political and military situation in Prague. At 02:41 on 7 May, a German delegation signed an act of unconditional surrender at Reims. Fighting was to end on all fronts at 23:01 hours Central European Time on 8 May. German forces were to remain in the positions they occupied at that point. The capitulation represented the collapse of Dönitz's strategy of seeking a separate surrender in the West. At the same time, the Germans did what they could to save the armies in the East from Russian captivity. Jodl claimed that because of the uprising, it was impossible to order the troops in Bohemia/Moravia to capitulate. He asked the allies to send a message to the Czechs telling them to stop fighting and turn all transmitters over to the German Army.

German refugees in Old Town Square

This was an obvious attempt to stall for time. Eisenhower was not prepared to issue such an appeal but did agree to send a German staff officer under American escort both to Prague and to Schörner to deliver the terms of the capitulation. At the same time he made preparations to order an advance on Prague if the Germans there continued fighting after midnight on 8 May.

Reuters announcement of the imminent German capitulation reached Prague on the morning of 7 May. But there was considerable confusion about what had been agreed at Reims. When Dönitz spoke on the German radio, he implied that the troops in the East were a barrier against Bolshevism and must continue the fight against the Russians. Orders issued at 01:35 on 7 May, five minutes after Jodl was authorized to sign a general capitulation, called for resistance in the East until the last second of the war: 'The aim is to pull back to the West everything possible from all fronts facing the eastern enemy and – if necessary – to fight your way through the Soviets.' As the War Diary of the

German Supreme Command noted, it was 'especially important' for Schörner's Army Group 'to keep up the fight' against the Russians 'for as long as possible' since this was the only way that German units would have any chance of reaching the Americans. Schörner's transmitter at Liblice thus denounced the news of a general capitulation as enemy propaganda : 'The Reich government has ceased to fight only against the Western powers. In our area the struggle will be continued until the Germans in the east are saved and until our way into the homeland is secured.'

On the afternoon of 7 May, however, four American tanks, led by Lieutenant-Colonel Pratt, the operations officer of V Corps, arrived in Prague. Pratt was escorting Colonel Meyer-Detring, the personal representative of Admiral Dönitz, who was carrying texts of the Reims agreement for Toussaint and Schörner. The American commander made it clear that Patton's forces would remain in Plzeň, leaving everything east of the demarcation line to the Red Army. The German emissary confirmed that the surrender terms signed at Reims applied to all fronts. German troops east of the Karlovy Vary–Plzeň–Budějovice line at midnight on 8 May would fall into Soviet hands. The news was officially broadcast by Kutlvašr at 23:15. For the first time everyone in the city finally realized that the US Third Army was not coming. The announcement came as a bombshell to Bunyachenko's men. The ČNR was unwilling to offer them asylum and the Red Army would take Prague. From monitoring radio traffic, Bunyachenko knew that Soviet armour was closing in on the city. His division must not be trapped. The role of his troops in saving the uprising would cut no ice with Stalin. The fate awaiting them at Soviet hands was indefinite detention in a labour camp or a shot in the back of the head. Bunyachenko had thus no option but to save his men by withdrawing as quickly as possible to the flimsy safety of American lines. Late on 7 May he ordered the division to break off the fighting and head towards Plzeň. By the early hours of 8 May, the Russians had gone. In the ČNR there were bitter recriminations in which the Communists were accused of freezing out Bunyachenko and leaving the population exposed to the SS terror. This, however, reckoned without the effect of Dönitz's surrender on the Germans.

On Tuesday 8 May, the bitterest fighting of the uprising took place with heavy shelling from German artillery on Letenské sady and air attacks on the barricades. Der Führer renewed its thrust across the Troja Bridge. Elements of the Milovice battle group reached Old Town Square, destroying the famous astrological clock and setting fire to the Old Town Hall with its priceless collection of medieval documents. Deprived of Bunyachenko's support, there was little poorly armed and untrained civilians could do against determined troops with armoured support. In the suburb of Krč the SS committed its worst atrocities. According to a police report, houses were burned and shops looted. Civilians were massacred indiscriminately. Many bodies lay in the streets and in a little church : 'They included men, women and even children from one to three years of age, all killed in a terrible way. Their heads and ears had been cut off, their eyes gouged out and their bodies run through and through with bayonets. There were pregnant women amongst them whose bodies had been ripped open.' These ghastly crimes were the work of 'young men between 17 and 20 years of age', crazed with vengeance as they fought the final battle of the Reich. Similar incidents occurred in Pankrác and elsewhere in the city.

But the military situation concealed German political weakness. If the struggle on all fronts was soon to end, there was no point in holding Prague and the lines of communication to Army Group Centre. The main task now was to reach the American lines before the surrender went into effect and the Red Army arrived. The Germans were thus no longer fighting to reconquer the city but to negotiate an agreement which would allow them to disengage and withdraw. Unlike the Vlasov Army they could not rely on Czech cooperation in an evacuation which would involve large numbers of wounded and civilians as well combat troops. While the SS was still advancing through the streets of the Old Town a new series of talks began. This time the German side asked only to be allowed to pull out of Prague unhindered and to gurantee the safety of German civilians. General Toussaint warned Kutlvašr that the alternative was the utter destruction of the city. Schörner had already issued the orders. The Czechs were prepared to make concessions to end the fighting. Isolated and short of weapons, they did not want Prague to suffer the fate of Warsaw in the last hours of the war.

German troops retreating from Prague on 8 May 1945

Toussaint, agreed to a temporary ceasefire while the details were worked out. This concession was offered over the objections of von Pückler who, in a drunken rage, drew his pistol and threatened to shoot his army colleague. In the confusion of the fighting, it was difficult to convey the news to the troops and Toussaint's son had to tour the streets at great personal risk, contacting each unit individually. By late afternoon, most outposts had obeyed the ceasefire order. The news, however, evidently did not reach the Luftwaffe for later that night the radio station was bombed. A final agreement was signed at 16:00 hours, calling for an armistice and an unopposed German withdrawal from Prague beginning at 18:00. While the Czechs opened the barricades, Toussaint was to render safe all mines and demolitions. He was also to take responsibility for dealing with any troops who refused to accept the agreement. The Germans were to leave their heavy equipment at the edge of the city and surrender the rest of their weapons just before the American demarcation line. German women and children were to be respected. Those unable to leave with the troops were to be handed over to the International Red Cross. As he signed the agreement, Toussaint, who spoke Czech and had served as military attaché at the German embassy before the war, apologized for the occupation and implied that his country deserved the ruin which it had now suffered : 'My nation is today the most wretched nation on earth. Its young people have been ruined by bad training for two generations. But gentleman, it is just, it is quite just.'

News of the ceasefire was broadcast by the Czech radio and the street loudspeaker system. The population was informed that the war was over and that they should fight the Germans only in self-defence. At the Czernin Palace there was great confusion. Frank was reluctant to leave the seat of his former glory and seemed divorced from reality. He did not finally set out until the early hours of the morning. There was a heated debate about the best route to the American lines. The direct road to Plzeň was occupied by Bunyachenko's retreating troops and some did not wish to risk a renewal of hostilities by using it as an evacuation route. In the end the Germans pulled out of Prague in two columns, guided through the barricades by Czech police. One took the direct route to Plzeň, risking confrontation with the Vlasov Army. The other went down the east bank of the Vltava where a massive military traffic jam developed south of the city. The following day this column was overrun by a Soviet armoured division and never reached the American lines. Army Group Centre, which had refused to surrender, was encircled and destroyed east of Prague, abandoned by Schörner who changed into civilian clothes and fled to Austria by plane.

While the Germans were still evacuating Prague, the first Soviet tanks appeared, entering the northern suburbs around 03:00 on 9 May. They were forward units of Koniev's army advancing from the Dresden area. The arrival of the Russians caused the collapse of the fragile ceasefire. Prague Radio urged the population to destroy the 'German murderers' and the rearguard was attacked. At 09:00 that morning German guns were still shelling Pankrác, the Old Town and the electricity generating station at Holešovice. Roving bands of SS were looting shops, firing at passersby and even attacking stray units of the German Army. One group, dug in at Olšany Cemetery, held out for several days and funerals had to take place under heavy military guard. Czech resistance fighters hunted down stragglers who were hanged from the lamp-posts and set on fire. In Prague-Motol, forty members of the Hitler Youth were butchered with knives and clubs before the eyes of other German prisoners. At his headquarters in Reims Eisenhower prepared to give the order for Patton to advance and impose order. But then the news arrived that the Red Army was in the city. Shortly after midday Koniev's troops were joined by elements of the 2nd Ukrainian Front from the east and the last pockets of Nazi resistance were overcome. There was rejoicing all over Prague as people crowded into the streets and squares to greet their Russian liberators and garland their tanks with flowers. The city had finally fallen but at the cost of 1,694 Czech dead. Jára Netušil, an employee of the Prague Electricity Company, who kept a diary in the chaotic final days of Nazi rule, noted with relief that at last 'it was all over'. But the long agony of Czechoslovakia had not yet ended.

'I wonder if we shall all go mad with freedom
and happiness when the war is over,
or whether we shall be too tired'

AN UNKNOWN CZECH SOLDIER : 1940

CHAPTER EIGHT

Aftermath

*A smashed bust of Hitler
on a Prague street
symbolizes the final end
of the Nazi occupation*

The Presidential cavalcade enters the First Courtyard of Prague Castle

ON 10 MAY 1945 part of the Czechoslovak government returned to Prague, landing at Ruzyně in a Soviet transport plane. The delegation was led by Zdeněk Fierlinger, the fellow-travelling Prime Minister, and the chairman of the Communist Party, Klement Gottwald. The next day the Czech National Committee formally surrendered its powers. In a speech to the nation, Gottwald proclaimed that Czechoslovakia had been freed from Nazi tyranny by Marshal Stalin and 'the glorious Red Army . . . The liberation from foreign rule opens up a new chapter in the history of our country. We must now lay firm foundations for a new and happy life in a free, really democratic, truly people's Czechoslovakia and never allow a return to the pre-Munich days.' On 18 May President Beneš came back to his liberated capital, entering the Hradčany for the first time since the dark days of October 1938. The packed streets were decorated with huge portraits of Beneš and Stalin. From every lamp-post and window the Soviet flag flew beside the national colours of free Czechoslovakia. Pro-Western groups which had hoped for liberation by the Americans had been disappointed. Eisenhower had surrendered Bohemia/Moravia to the Soviet sphere of influence. The Communists, already established in key ministries of the Košice government, were able to consolidate their position in the post-war period. The power of the Russians and their Czech Communist allies was immediately evident. The Czech Brigade in the West, which had been besieging Dunkirk in the closing months of the war, was refused entry into the Soviet zone. It was allowed to participate in the victory parade in Prague but was ordered back to Plzeň two days later. This was a clear attempt to keep an armed force linked with the West away from the centre of power, and a symbol of what was to come.

The Red Army immediately claimed the credit for saving Prague, beginning the process which consigned both the Vlasov Army and the Anglo-Americans to the dustbin of history. When Beneš made his first speech in his liberated capital, he emphasized the contribution of all the allies to final victory. He was followed by Fierlinger who reserved his praise for the achievments of the Red Army. In July 1945 the Soviet newspaper *Izvestia* ran a series entitled 'In the heart of Europe' which opened with an article on the battle for Prague. It praised Czech bravery but nowhere admitted that help would have come from the West if the Russians had not asked Eisenhower to halt Patton's advance. The impression was given that Czech appeals had been heard 'only in Moscow and that the Red Army overcame great physical and military obstacles to reach Prague on time.' This soon became the official line of

the Czech Communist Party. As its newspaper, *Rudé Právo,* remarked in January 1948 : 'The (US) 3rd Army ... stood in Czechoslovakia armed to the teeth ... while the uprising was drowned in blood. All Prague saw the Soviet tanks but there was no one who had seen American and English tanks near Prague. Why? Those who consider it their duty to rehabilitate their overseas protectors explain it by the existence of a "demarcation line." When one wants to help people in danger "demarcation lines" do not exist.' The following month the Communists seized total power and this version was established as historical truth. The legend was also promoted by Moscow in articles and movies. In May 1968, during the Prague Spring, the Czech old guard complained to the Russians about a proposed film on the US liberation of Plzeň, claiming that by authorizing such projects, the Dubček regime was in danger 'of forgetting the sacrifices made by the Soviet Union to liberate Czechoslovakia'. The issue was considered important enough for discussion by Brezhnev and the presidium of the Soviet Communist Party.

The decision to halt the US advance at Plzeň has remained controversial ever since. Patton, who finally reached Prague as a tourist on 27 July 1945, believed that Eisenhower had made a mistake. Many contemporaries agreed. As early as 18 May 1945, an Anglo-

First-day covers celebrating the return of President Beneš. The photograph depicts the Old Town Hall which was badly damaged during the Prague Uprising

on Prague. And would his strategy have made any real difference to post-war politics in Czechoslovakia? The Soviet Union was popular with the Czechs because it was uncontaminated by implication in the betrayal at Munich in September 1938. Moreover Beneš had already conceded a preponderance of power to the Communists at Košice in March 1945, weeks before his government returned to Prague. In this situation it is unclear what real difference the arrival of the Americans would have made. The Czechs, unlike the Poles, had still to experience the reality of Soviet power, a lesson that was not really learned until after the Communist coup of February 1948 when it was already too late.

In the aftermath of liberation old scores were settled with the Nazis and their Czech collaborators. Thousands of Germans were detained under horrifying conditions in state, municipal and police prisons all over Prague. More than 5000 were crammed into the corridors of the Strahov sports stadium. The prisoners were painted with swastikas and forced to clear the barricades and bury the dead. They were beaten up and spat upon. Every evening Russian soldiers broke into the detention centres to rape and loot. Conditions in Prague became so bad as to threaten public health and the detainees were evacuated to the former ghetto at Terezín, where they were given the same rations

Troops of the Czechoslovak Army in the East at a victory parade in Wenceslas Square

as Jewish victims of the Nazis. No attempt was made to separate the innocent from the guilty. Such excesses were repeated all over the liberated territory. A later investigation by the Czechoslovak government found 3000 cases of maltreatment, certainly an underestimate, all of which had taken place between May and July 1945 'in the aftermath of military and revolutionary actions against the Germans motivated by recollections of recent atrocities committed by the German administration'. In 1946 over a million Germans were expelled from Czechoslovakia. As Beneš argued in June 1945, before Munich the Sudetens had been offered tolerance and forgiveness: 'The world today knows the German answer to this appeal of mine; their answer spelt terror, treason, concentration camps for us Czechs... Can it therefore surprise anybody in the whole world when we say that we are determined to get rid of these Germans forever?' The empty villages in the Sudetenland, the abandoned apartments in Prague and elsewhere, were taken over by Czechs. The hatred created by Frank had rebounded on his own people and he spent his last days lamenting their tragic fate.

In the first weeks of peace, unofficial people's courts exercised summary justice on suspected collaborators. Many old personal scores were paid off in the process. The actress, Adina Mandlová, was held in Pankrác Prison, accused of having taken German citizenship during the war. The real reason, however, was her alleged relationship with Frank. Conditions in the jail were appalling, with suspects crammed into small cells without proper sanitation. Ironically the Czech jailers had served under the old regime and copied the SS in their treatment of the prisoners. There was no documentary evidence against Mandlová, but when she complained about her continued detention she was told: 'What do you expect? This is a revolution.' Mandlová believed that she, along with the director of the National Theatre, Václav Talich, and the comedian, Vlasta Burian, had been made scapegoats for the entire community: 'Somebody had to pay to give the crowd satisfaction.' The cameramen, stuntmen, directors and producers at Barrandov were never accused of collaboration, although they had worked under German supervision throughout the occupation. The musicians at the National Theatre who had played for Goebbels, never went to prison. On a wider scale nobody asked the Communists what they had been doing during the period of the Nazi-Soviet Pact or criticised the workers for producing guns for the Reich. Denunications to the 'people's courts' were often made by those with most to hide, who had wrapped themselves in the flag of patriotism in the last days of the war. Heda Margolius Kovaly, who had survived the Nazi concentration camps, was shocked by the mood of the nation in this period. It was her 'first frightening glimpse of the devastation, the deep corrosion that the war had inflicted upon us. It had divided people like the slash of a knife, and that wound would take a long time to heal.'

Members of the Protectorate government were rounded-up and detained in Pankrác Prison while their cases were investigated. The Minister of Education and Propaganda, Emmanuel Moravec, committed suicide to avoid arrest and trial. Many suspected, however, that he had been murdered because he knew too much. Hácha never faced a court. A sick and broken man, vilified for his

Cheering crowds welcome the arrival in Prague of the Czechoslovak Army in the West

errors in the political and military judgements of General Marshall and General Eisenhower'. This, however, ignores the context in which the decisions were taken, in particular the demands of global strategy. Before the testing of the atomic bomb in July 1945, the Americans believed that they needed Soviet participation in the war against Japan to keep down their own casualties in Asia and were unwilling to take any step that might alienate Moscow. As for Prague, if the Russians wanted to lose lives for the sake of a prestige victory, that was up to them. Few Americans were prepared to risk losses amongst their own troops in the last days of the war. In this respect, Churchill was asking someone else to pay the price of an advance

Czech who had spent the war in the capital claimed that people had eagerly awaited liberation from the West. But they had been 'tremendously disappointed' when the Americans simply looked on while Prague experienced the final agonies of the Nazi occupation. An SOE officer, who managed to penetrate the Soviet road blocks which quickly cut the city off from the US zone around Plzeň, recorded a similar impression, noting the disappointment of non-Communist resistance groups at the lack of support from the West. The Communists were already making political capital from the claim that cries for help had been heard 'only in Moscow, [while] the West turned a deaf ear'. According to Beneš' secretary, Eduard Táborský, the exile President's 'bitterest disappointment came in the spring of 1945 when General Patton's armies were ordered to halt . . . Had Patton continued to advance he could have liberated not only Prague but the whole of Bohemia and a substantial portion of Moravia. The Communists would have been denied the advantage conferred by the presence and active support of the Red Army and the NKVD [secret police] in entrenching themselves in the most populous and most strategic areas of Czechoslovakia.'

The Czech exile historian Radomír Luža, writing in 1984, endorsed this judgement, arguing that Prague 'was lost to the West by

President and Mrs Beneš return to Prague on 16 May 1945. Beneš' face shows the strain of war and exile

capitulation to Hitler in March 1939, he died in prison when the medicine he required for a diabetic condition was refused. The Minister of Industry and Labour, Bertsch, the agent of SS industrial strategy, was sentenced to life imprisonment and died behind bars. Frank, who had fled to Plzeň with his wife in an armoured limousine filled with suitcases, was detained by the Americans. In a petulant letter to his captors he complained that his luggage had been confiscated and that he had not enjoyed a proper wash for two days. He asked for a razor, a clean shirt and an English phrase book. He did not need the last item, however, for his stay with the Americans was brief. Handed over to the Czechs, Frank was tried for his crimes and hanged at Pankrác Prison on 22 May 1946. Daluege, Heydrich's successor as acting Reichsprotektor, met a similar end. Hitler's first and last viceroys in Prague, Konstantin von Neurath and Wilhelm Frick, were tried with the surviving Nazi leaders by the International Military Tribunal at Nürnberg. Neurath was sentenced to fifteen years in prison. Frick received the death penalty. Karl Henlein, the Gauleiter of the Sudetenland, who had played a leading role in the destruction of the pre-war Czechoslovak state, called for resistance to the last round before surrendering to the Americans. But he slashed his wrists with a razor blade when it became obvious that he would be handed over to the Czechs.

Nor did the Americans offer asylum to the German garrison of Prague and the survivors of Army Group Centre. The troops who reached the demarcation line were turned back to the Red Army. SS Gruppenführer von Pückler shot himself on 10 May 1945. He was a wanted man who could expect no mercy from the Russians. He had served on the Eastern front as Höhere SS und Polizei Führer with Army Group Centre in 1942 and later commanded a Waffen SS division composed of Latvian volunteers. General Toussaint was given life by a Prague court in October 1948. The charges included his espionage activities as military attaché before

K. H. Frank faces the death penalty

The memorial plaque on the St Cyril and St Methodius Church on Resslova Street by the Czech sculptor Franta Belsky

Munich as well as his role during the Prague uprising. The most tragic fate of all was reserved for the Vlasov Army. On 10 May 1945 the wounded left behind in Prague hospitals were dragged from their beds by soldiers of the Red Army and shot without trial. One hundred and eighty-seven were buried in a mass grave in Olšany Cemetery. The graves of the others were scattered through the western suburbs of Prague. The rest of the 1st Division reached the Americans, but was surrendered to Soviet justice. Those who did not commit suicide were shot as traitors or transported to the labour camps and an unknown end. The senior officers, including Vlasov and Bunyachenko, were tried for

The remains of a Lidice house

treason and condemned to death in Moscow on 2 August 1946. The vital role of the 1st Division in saving Prague from the SS terror was erased from both Czech and Soviet history.

The Germans and Czechs condemned for their role in the Protectorate, however, were soon joined by many of those who had resisted them. After the Communist seizure of power in 1948, General Kutlvašr was arrested and spent years in prison along with many others who had fought in the West or belonged to the non-Communist resistance. He found himself cleaning out the prison latrines with his former German opponent, General Toussaint. Beneš' military represen-

tative on the ČNR, Captain Nechanský, was executed after the coup. Professor Pražák also found himself in trouble for signing a ceasefire with the fascist enemy on 8 May 1945. Even the Communists on the ČNR, like Smrkovský, found themselves under a cloud for compounding with the Nazis. This was merely the prelude to a rewriting of history which marginalized the non-Communist resistance and elevated the Communist Party of Czechoslovakia into the true champions of the national idea, an ironic development in view of the notorious deference of Gottwald and his successor, Novotný, to Moscow. Pro-Western groups and the pre-Košice exile government under Beneš were denounced as tools of Anglo-American imperialism. If anyone noted the parallel with Nazi propaganda, they found it wise to remain silent.

A final judgement on the wartime period suggests that the experience of Munich and the Nazi occupation, profoundly disillusioned many Czechs with the West and the democratic ideals of Tomáš Masaryk. As one observer remarked, people had become accustomed to obeying orders. Abandoned by Britain and France at Munich, the Czechs found themselves further isolated by an Anglo-American strategy that relegated them to a low priority and created a sense of national isolation. In this situation, only the Soviet Union and its Czech Communist allies seemed to offer a means of national salvation. The Communists capitalized on this in 1945, exploiting the final betrayal by a US army which stood idle in Plzeň while Czechs struggled and died. The occupation had also created a regimented and conformist society which did not encourage civic responsibility or involvement. For many passivity, seeking refuge from the outside world in a private 'inner space', had become deeply ingrained. All of this was exploited by the Communists in the post-war years, when they drew a veil of silence over the complexities of life under the occupation, while offering a heroic myth of working-class resistance under the leadership of the Soviet Union and the Communist Party. At the same time they quietly incorporated many of the worst aspects of the Nazi system, adapting the Gestapo informer network for their own purposes. In many ways, including its cultivation of the working class, its war against the intellectuals, even its appeal to anti-Semitism in the show trials of Slánský and other Jewish Communists, the new totalitarian system had many echoes of the occupation regime.

In 1946 the radical British historian, A. J. P. Taylor, visited Prague and spent several hours with Beneš at the Hradčany. During their conversation, the President led Taylor to a window and gestured at the spires and rooftops below: 'Is it not beautiful?' he asked. 'The only undamaged city in Central Europe and all my doing.' But the price had been high. As Táborský argued, the bloodless Communist coup in February 1948 could only be understood by reference to the events of September 1938, March 1939 and May 1945: 'The Munich betrayal, the twilight existence leading up to Hitler's *coup de grace* of March 1939, and the long ordeal of Nazi oppression had shattered the Czechoslovak people's morale . . . Even under the most propitious circumstances it would have taken some time for them to reestablish their confidence and spirit. When, instead of finding the freedom from fear which they had longed for, they were subjected to the Communist variety of intimidation and lawlessness, the shock was too much for them and their civic courage slipped to an all-time low.' Some reverted to an opportunist policy of collaboration whilst others stood back and waited for somebody else to produce a miracle. In 1940 a Czech exile had wondered whether the nation would go mad with joy after liberation or whether everyone would be too tired. His question had now been answered in full.

The cover of a pro-Soviet propaganda book cover showing a Cossack watering his horse beneath Charles Bridge. The caption reads 'For All Eternity'

A postcard of May 1945 featuring portraits of President Beneš (right) and Joseph Stalin (left) - a sinister portent of things to come

APPENDIX

The book is based on numerous sources in several languages, both published and unpublished, and extensive interviews. Of particular importance amongst the published works on the Protectorate are Detlef Brandes, *Die Tschechen unter Deutschem Protektorat* (München and Wien 1969), Vojtěch Mastný, *The Czechs under Nazi Rule: The Failure of National Resistance* (New York 1971), Sheila Grant Duff, *A German Protectorate: The Czechs under Nazi Rule* (London 1942), and the essays in Miroslav Rechcigl (ed), *Czechoslovakia Past And Present*, vol. 1 (The Hague 1968). An invaluable insight into the experience of the German occupiers is offered by Wilhelm Dennler's memoir, *Die bohemische Passion* (Freiburg 1953), an account by a bureaucrat in the Reichsprotektor's office based on diaries he kept at the time. A biography of Reichsprotektor von Neurath by John L. Heinemann, *Hitler's First Foreign Minister* (Stanford 1979), contains extensive information on the early years of the Protectorate although Heinemann is too kind to his subject.

Documentary accounts from the Czech side include, Čestmír Amort, *Heydrichiáda* (Prague 1965), Václav Král, *Lesson from History* (Prague 1962) and Jiří Doležal and Jan Křen, *Czechoslovakia's Fight 1938-1945: Documents on the Resistance* (Prague 1964), although all are marred by their Communist bias. Král also wrote *Pravda o okupaci* (Prague 1962), a standard Communist account of the Protectorate. Books on the Heydrich episode and its aftermath include Callum MacDonald, *The Killing of SS Obergruppenführer Reinhard Heydrich* (London 1989). A particularly stimulating essay on the assassination by Jaroslav Drábek, 'The Assassination of Reinhard Heydrich: A Reevaluation', is contained in the Rechcigl volume cited above. The operations of the Czechoslovak parachute groups from Britain are examined by Jiří Šolc, *Bylo málo mužů* (Prague 1990). The story of the resistance is comprehensively covered by Václav Černý in *Pláč koruny české* (Toronto 1977). Information on the activities of the Gestapo is contained in Jiří Šolc, *Ďáblova past* (Prague 1993) and an article by Stanislav Berton, 'Das Attentat auf Reinhard Heydrich von 27 Mai 1942. Ein Bericht des Kriminalrats Heinz Pannwitz' in *Vierteljahreshefte für Zeitgeschichte*, volume 33, 1985. The role of the Vlasov Army in the Prague Uprising is authoritatively set out by Stanislav Auský in *Vojska generála Vlasova v Čechách* (Toronto 1980). The Uprising and its aftermath are also discussed in Josef Slanina and Zdeněk Vališ, *Generál Karel Kutlvašr* (Praha 1993). Of particular importance on the experience of Czech Jews under occupation are H. G. Adler, *Theresienstadt* (Berlin 1960), Heda Margolius Kovaly, *Prague Farewell* (London 1988), Ezra Mendelsohn, *The Jews of East Central Europe* (Bloomington 1984), and the essays in Avigor Dagan (ed), *The Jews of Czechoslovakia* (New York 1984). The operations of Nazi courts are discussed in Ingo Müller, *Hitler's Justice the Courts of the Third Reich* (London 1991). The Prague psychiatrist, Vladimír Vondráček, gives a fascinating account of everday life under the Germans in *Konec vzpomínání 1938-1945* (Praha 1988). The activities of high society are covered in the memoirs of the film star, Adina Mandlová, *Dneska už se tomu směju* (Toronto 1976). Further information on Czech cinema under occupation can be found in Josef Škvorecký, *All The Bright Young Men and Women: A Personal History of Czech Cinema* (Toronto 1971).

The photographs in the text come from the Kaplan/MacDonald Archive and private collections. They are reproduced here with the help of Alan Watson of the University of Warwick, Coventry, England. Stasz Gnych of Brown Packaging provided enouragement and guidance during the composition of the book. The authors would like to thank the following individuals for their assistance during the research for the book: Stanislav Auský, Viktor Faktor, Dr Stanislav Kokoška of the Czech Army Historical Institute, Hana Mašková, Jakub Outrata, Hana Outratová, Rudolf Pernický and Father Jaroslav Šuvarský in Prague; Phil Nix in Birmingham; Rabbi Albert Friedlander, Joe Susser and Sir Peter Wilkinson in London; Dr George Ženatý in New York, whose encyclopaedic knowledge of the period is unsurpassed; Dr Eduard Táborský in Austin, Texas; Josef Škvorecký of Toronto, Canada; George J. Kovtun of the European Division, Library of Congress, Washington DC; and Jaroslav Čvančara.

WARWICK AND LONDON
JUNE 1994

CALLUM MacDONALD
JAN KAPLAN

REFERENCES

CHAPTER ONE/ HITLER OVER PRAGUE

The quotation on the chapter heading is from Czechoslovak Ministry of Foreign Affairs Department of Information, *Four Fighting Years* (London and New York 1943), p. 21

The first quotation on page 19 is from *The Times*, 15 March 1939, p. 14

The second quotation on page 19 is from Callum MacDonald, *The Killing of SS Obergruppenführer Reinhard Heydrich* (London 1989), p. 59

The third quotation on page 19 is from Detlef Brandes, *Die Tschechen unter deutschem Protektorat*, vol 1 (Munich and Vienna 1969), p. 18

The quotation on page 20 is from *Documents on German Foreign Policy*, Series D (Washington 1949-1958), vol 4, p. 270

The first quotation on page 21 is from George Kennan, *From Prague after Munich* (Princeton 1968), p. 85

The second quotation on page 21 is from MacDonald, p. 61

The quotations on page 22 are from Kennan, p. 87

The quotation on page 30 is from Vojtěch Mastný, *The Czechs under Nazi Rule* (New York and London 1971), p. 58

The first quotation on page 31 is from *The Times*, 30 November 1939, p. 7

The east quotations on page 31 are from Sheila Grant Duff, *A German Protectorate : The Czechs Under Nazi Rule* (London 1970), pp. 51-2

The quotation on page 32 is from Kennan, p. 116

The quotation on page 33 is from *The Times*, 16 March 1939, p. 14

The quotation on page 37 is from Kennan, p. 104

The quotation on page 39 is from *Ibid.* pp. 111-13

The first quotation on page 40 is from *The Times*, 6 April 1939, p. 11

The second quotation on page 40 is from Sir Paul Dukes, *An Epic of the Gestapo* (London 1940), pp. 52-3

The first quotation on page 41 is from Kennan, pp. 157-9

The second quotation on page 41 is from *Ibid.* p. 209

The third quotation on page 41 is from *The Times*, 20 July 1939, p. 13

The fourth quotation on page 41 is from *Ibid.* 18 June 1939, p. 8

The first two quotations on page 42 are from Kennan, p. 211

The third quotation on page 42 is from *The Times*, 6 June 1939, p. 14

The quotation on page 44 is from Kennan, p. 118

CHAPTER TWO/ THE NEW MASTERS

The quotation on the chapter heading is from John Keegan (ed), *The Goebbels Diaries 1939-1941* (London 1982), p. 166

The quotation on page 48 is from Duff, p. 267

The quotation on page 50 is from Brandes, p. 87

The quotation on page 51 is from *Goebbels*, pp. 34-5

The first quotation on page 54 is from *Ibid.* p. 52

The second quotation on page 54 is from John L. Heinemann, *Hitler's First Foreign Minister Konstantin von Neurath Diplomat and Statesman* (Stanford 1979), p. 204

The third quotation on page 54 is from *Goebbels Diary*, p. 69

The fourth quotation on page 54 is from *Ibid.* pp. 34-5

The first quotation on page 55 is from Duff, p. 276

The second quotation on page 55 is from *Ibid.*, pp. 241-43

The quotation on page 57 is from MacDonald, pp. 83-84

The first quotation on page 58 is from *Goebbels Diary*, p. 356

The first quotation on page 59 is from Duff, pp. 246-7

The second quotation on page 59 is from Brandes, p. 214

The first quotation on page 61 is from K. H. Frank, 'Tschechischer Legionargeist - oder Friede im Protektorat', *Böhmen und Mähren*, January 1941, pp. 12-14

The next two quotations on page 61 are from Duff, pp. 178-9

The last quotation on page 61 is from Mastný, p. 173

The quotation on page 64 is from 'Memo by Lockhart', 25 July 1941, C8441/57/12 F0371/36381, Foreign Office Papers, Public Record Office, London.

CHAPTER THREE/ SS CITY

The quotation on the chapter heading is from Král, p. 114

The quotation on page 73 is from J. B. Hutak, *With Blood and with Iron: The Lidice Story* (London 1957), p. 44

The first quotation on page 76 is from Král, p. 138

The second quotation on page 76 is from Norman Cameron and R. H. Stevens (translators), *Hitler's Table Talk 1941-1944* (London 1953), pp. 237-8

The third quotation on page 76 is from Louis Lochner (ed), *The Goebbels Diary* (London 1948), p. 51

The quotation on page 77 is from MacDonald, p. 136

The quotation on page 82 is from Eugene Davidson, *The Trial of the Germans* (New York 1966), p. 280

The first quotation on page 84 is from MacDonald, p. 198

The second quotation on page 84 is from Michael Burleigh, *Germany Turns Eastwards Ostforschung in the Third Reich* (Cambridge 1989), p. 297

The quotation on page 86 is from Erich Kulka, 'Jews in the Czechoslovak Armed Forces in World War Two' in Avigdor Dagan (ed), *The Jews of Czechoslovakia*, vol. 3 (New York 1984), p. 403

The first quotation on page 88 is from MacDonald, p. 204

The second quotation on page 88 is from *Ibid.* p. 205

The quotation on page 89 is from Radomír Luža, *The Transfer of the Sudeten Germans* (New York and London 1964), p. 257

The quotation on page 90 is from Jiří Doležal and Jan Křen (eds), *Czechoslovakia's Fight Documents on the Resistance Movement of the Czechoslovak People* (Prague 1964), p. 104

CHAPTER FOUR/ THE PALACE OF DEATH

The quotation on the chapter heading is from Sir Paul Dukes, *An Epic of the Gestapo* (London 1940), pp. 182-3

The first three quotations on page 95 are from Duff, pp. 55-7

The next two quotations on page 95 are from Ingo Müller, *Hitler's Justice: The Courts of the Third Reich* (Cambridge Mass. 1991), pp. 154-58

The sixth quotation on page 95 is from *Ibid.* p. 130

The last quotation on page 95 is from Král, p. 157

The first quotation on page 96 is from Müller, p. 167

The second quotation on page 96 is from Müller, p. 109

The quotation on page 97 is from Stanislav Hlaváček, *Pečkárna* (Prague No. Date), p. 5

The first quotation on page 98 is from Müller, p. 142

The remaining quotations on page 98 are from Günther Deschner, *Heydrich: The Pursuit of Total Power* (London 1981), pp. 200-1

The quotations on page 100 are from George Bilainkin, *Second Diary of a Diplomatic Correspondent* (London 1946), pp. 269-70

The last quotation on page 100 os from Ivan Peterman, 'Prague's Four Fantastic Days', *Saturday Evening Post*, 14 July 1945, pp. 20-1

The first quotation on page 101 is from Bilainkin, p. 270

The second quotation on page 101 is from Böhme's party file, Berlin Documents Centre

The first quotation on page 102 is from Dukes, pp. 182-3

The second quotation on page 102 is from interview with Dr J. Ženatý

The first quotations on page 103 are from Duke, p. 97

The last quotation on page 103 is from Adina Mandlová, *Dneska už se tomu směju* (Toronto 1976), p. 165

The quotation on page 104 is from Duke, p. 90

The first quotation on page 105 is from Mastný, p. 78

The second quotation on page 105 is from Vladimír Vondráček, *Konec vzpomínání 1938-1945* (Praha 1988), p. 222

The third and fourth quotations on page 105 are from Czechoslovak Ministry of Foreign Affairs Department of Information, *Four Fighting Years* (London and New York 1943), p. 138

The last quotation on page 105 is from Král, p. 145

The quotation on page 109 is from interview with Dr J. Ženatý

The first quotation on page 110 is from *Goebbels*, p. 167

The second quotation on page 110 is from interview with Dr J. Ženatý

The third quotation on page 110 is from Bilainkin, p. 291

The first quotation on page 112 is from Král, pp. 157-8

The second quotation on page 112 is from Dukes, p. 168

CHAPTER FIVE/
THE PRAGUE JEWS

The quotation at the chapter heading is from Václav Král, *Lesson from History* (Prague 1962), p. 126

The quotation on page 116 is from Kennan, p. 37

The quotation on page 117 is from Sheila Grant Duff, *A German Protectorate the Czechs under Nazi Rule* (London 1970), p. 136

The quotation on page 118 is from Gerald Reitlinger, *The Final Solution* (London 1971), pp. 24-5

The first quotation on page 121 is from MacDonald, p. 40

The second quotation on page 121 is from Král, p. 126

The quotation on page 125 is from Heda Margolius Kovaly, *Prague Farewell* (London 1988), p. 8

The first quotation on page 126 is from Livia Rothkirchen, 'The Jews of Bohemia and Moravia 1938-1945' in Avigdor Dagan (ed), *The Jews of Czechoslovakia*, vol. 3 (New York 1984), p. 33

The second quotation on page 126 is from Kovaly, p. 9

The quotation on page 128 is from Joseph C. Pick, 'The Story of the Czech Scrolls', in Dagan, p. 586

The first quotation on page 132 is from Martin Gilbert, *The Holocaust: The Jewish Tragedy* (London 1987), p. 364

The remaining quotations on page 132 are from Dewey W. Linze, *The Trial of Adolf Eichmann* (Los Angeles 1961), p. 121

The first quotation on page 134 is from Zdeněk Lederer, 'Terezín' in Dagan, pp. 151-2

The second quotation on page 134 is from Gilbert, p. 792

The third quotation on page 134 is from Linze, p. 224

CHAPTER SIX/
OCCUPATIONAL HAZARDS

The quotation on the chapter heading is from Heda Margolius Kovaly, *Prague Farewell* (London 1988), pp. 31-2

The first quotation on page 138 is from Mandlová, p. 117

The second quotation on page 138 is from Karel Holbek, 'The Years of German Occupation' in Miroslav Rechcigl (ed), *Czechoslovakia Past and Present,* vol. 1 (The Hague 1968), p. 260

The quotation on pages 144 is from Kovaly, p. 37

The quotation on page 147 is from MacDonald, p. 136

The first quotation on page 148 is from *Four Fighting Years,* pp. 83-4

The second quotation on page 148 is from Detlev J. K. Peukert, *Inside Nazi Germany Conformity. Opposition and Racism in Everyday Life* (London 1987), p. 78

The first quotation on page 154 is from *Goebbels Diary,* p. 124

The second quotation on page 154 is from *Filmový kurýr,* 23 March 1939

The quotation on page 155 is from Leni Riefenstahl, *The Sieve of Time* (London 1992), p. 297

The quotation on page 156 is from Mandlová, p. 124

The quotations on page 158 are from *Ibid.*

CHAPTER SEVEN/
THE HOUR HAS COME

The quotation on the chapter heading is from Král, p. 161

The quotations on page 163 are from Brandes, p. 107

The quotation on page one 164 is from Czech Intelligence Summary Number 28, N705/707/12 FO 371/47124, Public Record Office, London

The quotation on page 165 is from *The Times,* 23 April 1945, p. 4

The first quotations on page 169 are from *Ibid.,* 4 May 1945, p. 4

The last quotation on page 169 is from Churchill to Ismay for Chiefs of Staff, 24 April 1945, N4548/650/12 F0371/47121, Public Record Office, London

The first quotation one page 170 is from Forrest C. Pogue, *US Army in World War II. European Theater of Operations The Supreme Command,* (Washington 1964), p. 469

The second quotation on page 170 is from Sargent to Churchill, 6 May 1945, N5307/207/12 F0371/47086, Public Record Office, London

The first quotation on page 173 is from Eduard Táborský, *President Eduard Beneš between East and West 1938-1948* (Stanford 1981), p. 212

The second quotation on page 173 is from Doležal and Křen, pp. 104-5

The quotation on page 177 is from John Erickson, *The Road to Berlin* (London 1985), p. 849

The first quotation on page 180 is from Doležal and Křen, p. 109

The second quotation on page 180 is from Král, p. 161

The third quotation on page 180 is from Brandes, p. 132

The first quotation on page 184 is from *The Times,* 7 May 1945, p. 4

The second quotation on page 184 is from interview with Dr J. Ženatý

The third quotation on page 184 is from Charles Whiting, *Patton's Last Battle* (New York 1987), p. 175

The fourth quotation on page 184 is from Erich Kulka, 'Jews in the Czechoslovak Armed Forces in World War Two' in Dagan, p. 423

The fifth quotation on page 184 is from Alexander for Chiefs of Staff, 4 January 1945, N259/259/12 FO 371/47099, Public Record Office, London

The quotations on page 191 are from Joachim Schultz-Naumann, *The Last Thirty Days : The War Diary of the German Armed Forces High Command From April to May 1945* (London 1991), p. 72 & p. 77

The first quotation on page 192 is from *The Times,* 7 May 1945, p. 6

The second quotation on page 192 is from Radomír Luža, *The Transfer of the Sudeten Germans* (London 1964), pp. 260-61

The first quotation on page 194 is from 'March of Time' Cameraman's Dope Sheet, L-54, Library of Congress, Washington DC.

The second quotation on page 194 is from Jára Netušil 'Manuscript Diary.' In possession of authors

CHAPTER EIGHT/ AFTERMATH

The quotation on the chapter heading is from Duff, pp. 241-3

The east quotation on page 197 is from Doležal and Křen, p. 111

The second quotation on page 197 is from Roberts to Foreign Office, 30 July 1945, N9459/5217/12 F0371/47159, Public Record Office, London

The first quotation on page 198 is from Luža, p. 259

The second quotation on page 198 is from Central Committee Archive, Moscow. I am grateful to John Crossland for this reference

The first two quotations on page 199 are from Memorandum by Allen, 18 May 1945, N5657/5217/12 F0371/47159, Public Record Office, London

The third quotation on page 199 is from Edward Táborský, 'The Triumph and Disaster of Eduard Beneš', *Foreign Affairs* July 1958, p. 680

The last quotation on page 199 is from Radomír Luža, 'The Liberation Of Prague: An American Blunder?,' *Kosmas Journal of Czechoslovak and Central European Studies,* vol. 3 Summer 1984, p. 45

The quotations on page 202 are from Luža, p. 269 and p. 273

The first two quotations on page 203 are from Mandlová, p. 163

The last quotation on page 203 is from Margolius, p. 53

The first quotation on page 206 is from Adam Sismann, *A.J.P. Taylor: A Biography* (London 1994), p. 163

The second quotation on page 206 is from Táborský, 'The Triumph and Disaster of Eduard Beneš', p. 681

The third quotation on page 206 is from Duff, p. 243

GERMAN AND PROTECTORATE GOVERNMENT OFFICES IN PRAGUE

(Present street names appear after Protectorate names)

RADIO
Reichs Radio Böhmen
- X Witoldstr. 1 - Vitoldova

REICHSPROTEKTOR
Hradčany Castle

OFFICES OF THE GERMAN STATE MINISTER FOR BOHEMIA/MORAVIA
German State Minister for Bohemia & Moravia - Czernin Palace
Military Plenipotentiary to State Minister - Platz der Wehrmacht - Vítězné nám.

MILITARY OFFICES IN PRAGUE
Army Administration for Reserve Troops - Platz der Wermacht - Vítězné nám.
Reserve Troops Inspection XIX Scharnhorstplatz 1/III - Nám. Svobody
Army Garrison Administration III Kleinseitner Ring - Malostranské nám.
Army HQ Prague III Kleinseitner Ring - Malostranské nám.
German Uniformed Police HQ - XIX General Roettig Str. 14 - Pelleova
Gestapo, Kripo & SD HQ - Petschek Palace - Bredauergasse - Politických vězňů

GERMAN LABOUR SERVICE OFFICES IN PRAGUE
German Labour Service Administration - Prague Castle
Main Labour Service Registation Office - XIX Scharnhorstplatz 1/III - Nám. Svobody
Labour Registration Office - Waldstein Palace

RED CROSS
German Red Cross Office Prague - Heydrich Ufer 4 – Smetanovo nábřeží

PRAGUE ADMINISTRATION
Acting Mayor of Prague - Town Hall - Old Town Sq
Prague Police HQ - I Viktoriastr. 15 - Národní třída

NAZI PARTY OFFICES
Area HQ - III Insel Kampa 506 - Kampa
German Labour Front
Womens Organization
Legal Service
Colonial League
German Civil Scrvants League
War Victims Relief Organization
Hitler Youth - IV Burgstädter Ring - Hradčanské nám.
German Girls League - II Rosengasse 5 - Růžová
SS Area HQ - II Nürnberger Str. 27 - Pařížská
SA Area HQ - II Stephangasse 36 - Štěpánská

CIVILIAN ORGANIZATIONS
German House - II Graben 26 - Na Příkopě
German Health Chamber
German News Service - II Beethovenstr. 5 - Opletalova

PROTECTORATE GOVERNMENT OFFICES
State President - Castle
Minister President - III Waldsteingasse Kolowrat Krakowsky Palace - Valdštejnská
Press Office of the Minister President - II Beethovenstr. 5 - Opletalova
Ministry of the Interior - VII Sommerberg Str. 67 - Milady Horákové
Ministry of Propaganda - III Waldsteingasse - Valdštejnská
II Beethovenstr. 5 - Opletalova

GERMAN THEATRES & CONCERT HALLS
New German Theatre - XII Richard Wagner Str. 7 - Wilsonova - Near Station
German Playhouse - I Obstmarkt - 540 Ovocný trh
Little Stage - Three Riders House - II Heuwaagsplatz 28 - Senovážné nám.
German Music Hall - II Klemensgasse 4 - Klimentská
Office for the Supervision of German Theatres in Prague - XII Rollergasse 3

GERMAN UNIVERSITY
German Charles University
German Technical High School - I Mozartplatz 2 - Nám. Jana Palacha
Nazi Student League - II Beethovenstrasse 38 - Opletalova

CALLUM MacDONALD & JAN KAPLAN

Prague

IN THE SHADOW OF THE SWASTIKA

HISTORICAL ADVICE DR TOMAN BROD and
MICHAL AJVAZ; PHOTOGRAPHS and
VISUAL MATERIAL FROM
KAPLAN/MacDONALD ARCHIVES; COVER
DESIGN JAN KAPLAN; GRAPHIC DESIGN
VLADIMÍR NÁROŽNÍK; IN THE EDITION
HISTORY and FACTS PUBLISHED IN 1995 BY
MELANTRICH, VÁCLAVSKÉ NÁMĚSTÍ 36,
112 12 PRAHA 1
EDITOR-IN-CHIEF DANA BRYNDOVÁ
TECHNICAL EDITOR KAMILA SCHÜLLEROVÁ
PRINTED BY POLYGRAFIA, a. s., PRAHA
AA 9,09; VA 38,53 (il. 26,86)
216 PAGES
FIRST EDITION

32-018-95